GROWING INTO LIFE

Long ago Job asked where can wisdom be found, only to discover that it came as gift through painful wrestling and persistent prayer.

In this remarkable book Janine demonstrates the continuing value of the timeless gift of wisdom which has been rooted in life, shaped by reflection, and formed in painful hope-filled prayer. She has known grief and clung on, held in the scarred but faithful hands of Christ; here she holds out a hand to us who find ourselves wanting to grow, whatever our circumstances, into the precious mystery of all that God calls us to be in Christ. This is a practical gem.

Rev. Mark Tanner, Warden, Cranmer Hall, St John's College, Durham University.

Wise, discerning, by turns both challenging and comforting, this book is a gift I would give to all the women whom I counsel. As a person who encounters people daily in need of spiritual guidance, I found it not simply insightful, but practical and compassionate. Janine invites her readers to take God seriously, to confront the issue of repressed emotions and trust that he cannot only heal, but transform our lives. She outlines the steps we need to take in order to see ourselves as God sees us. She does so by writing winsomely and persuasively. Anyone who reads this book with an open heart will find themselves challenged. But most of all, they will gain a new vision of God's invitation to all of us. To discover his goodness. And his love. I highly recommend it.

Dr. Bettina Collins, psychologist, ~~pastoral~~ and women's bible study lead⟨ ⟩ Southampton.

Janine's story of growth through events she would never have chosen provide inspiration, hope and practical tools for those whom themselves find life has not worked out as they had hoped or expected. She writes with honesty and integrity as she spells out how she has lived what she writes. Janine has refused to let her pain shape her image of God, but rather has let her image of God shape her pain. This book shows how she has done that. This book is no mere theory on spiritual growth - its been tried and tested in the furnace of pain, frustration and disappointment - and has been proved to bring about fruitfulness, lasting change and, most importantly of all, a deep and real imtimacy with a loving Heavenly Father.

Ness Wilson, church leader and public speaker.

This is a love story. Yes, it is a carefully crafted, clearly written and deeply reflective book about personal growth from a Christian perspective, filled with insights, wisdom and very real practical applications that will be truly life changing for those who listen to its voice and make it their own. But it is much more than that; it is a love story. Janine's understanding of 'growing into life' began when she fell in love with Richard. He started her on a journey of liberating self-discovery only to die suddenly nine years later leaving her a widow and mother of two small children. Out of trauma and grief the seeds that Richard had lovingly planted began to germinate leading her into a deeper love for God, for herself and those around her. This book has grown out of love and this is the gift that Janine offers us as readers.

Noel Moules, founder and director of the 'Workshop: Christian learning programme', a teacher, speaker, eco-peace activist and author of the book *Fingerprints of Fire, Footprints of Peace: a spiritual manifesto from a Jesus perspective.*

Growing into Life

Living by Design

Growing into Life
Living by Design

Janine Fair

Winchester, UK
Washington, USA

First published by Circle Books, 2012
Circle Books is an imprint of John Hunt Publishing Ltd., Laurel House, Station Approach,
Alresford, Hants, SO24 9JH, UK
office1@jhpbooks.net
www.johnhuntpublishing.com
www.circle-books.com

For distributor details and how to order please visit the 'Ordering' section on our website.

ISBN: 978 1 78099 411 6

A CIP catalogue record for this book is available from the British Library.

All scripture quotations are taken from the New International Version unless otherwise stated.

Design: Stuart Davies

Printed and bound in the USA by Edwards Brothers Malloy

We operate a distinctive and ethical publishing philosophy in all
areas of our business, from our global network of authors to
production and worldwide distribution.

CONTENTS

Also by Janine Fair

Surprised by grief - a journey into hope (IVP)

In memory of Richard, my growing partner
for almost 10 years.

ACKNOWLEDGMENTS

For every book that is written, there are a whole host of unsung heroes who tirelessly support the author in his or her task. This book is no exception, and I wish to thank several individuals for their part in helping me get to this point.

Firstly, I want to thank my two delightful children for their patience and love.

Secondly, I want to thank both my family and Richard's family for their support over the years.

Thirdly, I must express my gratitude to my long-suffering friends who have journeyed with me into growth and showered me with their love and care. In particular I want to thank Eva and Derek Leaf for their insightful comments during the shaping of this book, and Marie Birkinshaw for reading the final draft.

Finally, though, and most importantly, I want to thank God for his faithfulness, his provision, his protection and his love.

INTRODUCTION

Growing is an intensely personal journey, and the invitations we receive to embark upon it are, in many ways, unique. For some the invitation comes in the guise of an increasing sense of disillusionment and dissatisfaction with life, or a feeling of inner restlessness and yearning that needs to be explored. For others it takes the form of a sudden and painful change in circumstances, or a situation which causes them to be profoundly disturbed. To an extent the prelude to the invitation into growth is immaterial; what matters is that we accept it as a gracious gift from God, as an opportunity to learn and understand more of his love and grace. And yet acknowledging the story of our life up to this point is vitally significant, for it provides the background and context for our future building work and reminds us of the lessons that we have already learnt.

For me the invitation into growth came in the shape of a deepening relationship with Richard, the man who later became my husband. Through him God taught me about the importance of reflection, of listening to my emotions, and of taking responsibility for my own journey, as well as the pivotal role of other people in my growth.

It all began rather unexpectedly one autumn many years ago. I had just finished a year-long weekend bible school called 'Workshop', which had completely blown my mind. My previously unruffled vision of God had been irrevocably disturbed as I had begun to understand more of the awesome magnificence of his ways. I longed to learn more and so I decided to return the following year to help out as a volunteer.

From where I sat at the back of the hall, I had a perfect vantage point. I glanced down at my old notes as the teaching got underway, incredibly grateful for the opportunity to listen once again. The story of how a loving God had wrought his loving plans throughout the changing face of history was being told so passionately that my mind was quickly re-captivated. But even as my brain began to whir, I found myself experiencing a different pull. It seemed as if my gaze was being directed towards the latest newcomer to the course, a dark-haired man called Richard, seated in the second row.

The few words we exchanged at the break time left me feeling intrigued and wanting to know more. He possessed such an easy self-assurance and inner poise bordering on arrogance that piqued my natural curiosity. My head was buzzing with questions as he resumed his seat for the second session of the day. How could Richard be so sure of himself? And why did his self-confidence unsettle me so?

A chance meeting in a local shop a few days later gave me further cause for thought. I was defensive and rude, thrown off guard by seeing him out of context, and I quickly bailed out. But Richard had been listening attentively, and had picked up sufficient information to call on me at home later that week. There, as he proceeded to ply me and my housemates with incisive questions, I found my heart beginning to reel. Who was this man who could cut through my defenses with such alarming speed? And why did his questions provoke me so? I was gripped. This wasn't what I had anticipated at all. My neatly worked out arguments about the benefits of remaining single seemed to be flying in my face as he drew me on. And as he pressed me about my future plans, I realized that my assertion that I would end up serving God as a single medical missionary abroad was on increasingly shaky ground. Desperately I tried to get my thoughts in check before the next 'Workshop' weekend. Surely I was there to engage my mind, to satisfy my hunger to learn about God, and to fill my brain? I resented the emotional turbulence that this man, Richard, had provoked in me, and I was uncertain how to proceed. His sense of inner security was so powerful, so strong, that it exposed the huge anxiety and fearfulness I felt within.

I knew that God had been tenderly encouraging me to look inside for a while. The exercises I had undertaken as part of the course the previous year had begun to expose my impoverished self-esteem. Now it seemed as if God was gently beckoning me on to allow the head knowledge I had acquired to slowly permeate my heart. Suddenly it seemed as if my learning was taking on a more practical and emotive note.

As the weeks progressed and our time together became more frequent, I began to realize that Richard's probing questions were not designed to make me stumble and fall. Rather they were invitations for me to re-examine the fundamentals of my faith so that my understanding of myself and God could grow. It seemed that God did not want me to remain a captive to my fear, a fear that had led me to conclude that my usefulness to him lay purely in using my cognitive skills within my medical career. Rather he was interested in the whole of me and that included my heart. Now, in the warmth of the love that was developing for Richard, I was beginning to thaw and soften inside. I felt as if I was receiving God's unconditional love in tangible form through Richard's expressed love for me, and I found myself falling in love with God all over again.

Yet even as I relished the knowledge that God loved me exactly as I was, and the new found confidence that this security brought, I knew that God (and Richard) yearned for more. It was not enough to remain forever as I was right now; to do so would be to stagnate and slowly die inside. Rather God (and Richard) wanted me to develop and grow. I knew already that there was much within me that needed to change: learning to blend my life with Richard's was making me acutely aware of my many personal flaws. But whereas in the past I had imagined that God's love for me could be withdrawn if I displeased him in any way, now I began to appreciate the fact that his love for me would never fail. God's love was even more certain than the love that Richard now professed for me. And it was this awesome love that was inviting me to grow, in order that I might become more fully the person God had created me to be. God had made me as a unique one-of-a-kind being, and he didn't require me to fit into anyone else's shoes.

As I look back now on the early part of my relationship with Richard, I can see the seeds of growth beginning to form. At the time I was hungry for God and desperate to learn more of him. God answered that hunger by leading me firstly to the 'Workshop' course, and then by bringing Richard into my life. As I fell in love with Richard, in reality it was who God was wooing me to himself. My love for Richard was inextricably bound up in my love for God, and as I shared my heart with Richard, I became more able to open up to God. Despite all his imperfections, Richard showed me a pale reflection of the Father's unconditional love, a love that accepted me as I was at that moment, and yet constantly invited me to grow. I shall always be grateful to him for that.

A common feature of germination, however, is that the seeds themselves must die if the plant is to take on a life of its own. Sadly, this has been the case for me. Richard is no longer alive. He died suddenly in his sleep one night shortly after his fortieth birthday. I miss him still. The seeds of growth that were sown in the time I shared with Richard, in the warm soil of his love for me, are now starting to germinate.

Richard used to complain after we were married that he was then too close to be objective about my inner struggles. He knew that my reactions to his comments might produce uncomfortable repercussions for himself. Marriage to Richard did provide many of the raw materials for growth, especially as our two gorgeous children came along. There, in the busyness of life with two little ones, juggling the demands of Richard's role as a vicar in addition to my own work as a medical doctor, I learned very forcefully that I still had a lot of inner work to do. However, it was not until after Richard's death that I was able to realize the full impact of his legacy in my life: a passion for growing towards God. It took the fiery furnace of my grief to crack open the seeds that had been pressed down and trampled upon for some time.

This book is a result of that passion; it is a product of my growth. In it I will share the principles that I have learned as I have journeyed, in the hope that they will be of use to you. Throughout the book I will also allude to the details of my own personal journey, not as a blueprint for you to follow but in order to encourage you to engage more deeply with your own. However my greatest desire is that this book would serve as a signpost to awaken you to your own unique invitation into growth.

CHAPTER I

INVITATION INTO GROWTH

'And we, who with unveiled faces all reflect the Lord's glory, are being transformed into his likeness with ever-increasing glory, which comes from the Lord, who is the Spirit.' (2 Cor. 3.18)

Life on earth as we know it now is merely temporary. We must therefore use our time and energies wisely, to establish more of God's Kingdom in the here and now. The starting point must be our own life as we allow him to change us from deep within. However our growth is not a selfish aim: it is a process of mutual homecoming. As we come home to God and learn to be at home within our own unique expressions of humanity, we are then able to draw other people towards him.

The invitation

God wants everyone to grow. His desire is that we become more like him. He longs to transform the impoverished areas of our lives where we are in desperate need of him, and so he offers us an open-ended invitation to journey on the path of growth. This invitation surges like a strong and steady current through all the details of our lives. It beckons us to leave behind the safety of the riverbank and enter into the refreshing water of God's love and grace, so that he can transform us as we draw closer to him.

Like a repeated refrain within a musical symphony which brings a sense of form and unity to the whole, this invitation comes again and again, sometimes lilting softly and at other times clear and strong. It whispers to us in the darkness of night when our mind is full of anxiety and we are feverish with pain; and it shouts out for attention in the broad daylight when we attempt to silence it by keeping busy yet again. Each time the refrain returns it is subtly different, and yet the call behind the tune remains the same: to enter fully into the water of God's love and allow the current of our growth to draw us steadily towards him. It is a journey that impacts every aspect of our being, powerfully transcending the physical non-physical divide, as God empowers us to become more fully the people that he designed us to become.

The music of the king

Hearing this captivating melody as it invites us to journey into growth is itself a gift of God's grace. Only God can lift the deafness we have cultivated through years of neglect and disinterest, and revive our senses sufficiently so that we can respond to his alluring song. Max Lucado, in his allegorical story 'The song of the king'[1], captures this truth brilliantly. Three knights set out on a quest through a dark and dangerous forest to reach the king's castle. To guide them safely through, the king plays the same song on his flute three times a day from the castle wall. Each knight is allowed to take one travelling companion with him, and the prize is the hand of the king's daughter in marriage. The knight who eventually wins this quest is not the fastest or the strongest, much to everyone's surprise. Rather it is the one who chose the prince as his travelling companion, knowing that he alone would be able to teach him to recognize accurately the king's song.

Like those knights in Lucado's story, we too must learn to distinguish the music of the King. Our journey through life can feel quite dangerous as we negotiate our way through various twists and turns, and the only way to succeed is to walk in the company of Jesus, the King's son. The route that we must take through the dark forest does not always lead straight on; rather it can appear to be somewhat cyclical, as we go over similar ground again and again. It is as if we were travelling on a spiral pathway up a mountain, passing through different terrains as we cross each face of the slope. Densely wooded areas give way to scree-lined gradients, with grassy meadows and rushing rivers dotted in between. However the pathway of our growth calls us to keep on ascending the mountain as we ask God to reveal the best way to reach the top.

From time to time we will get weary, and need to rest to renew our energies before resuming the climb once again. Pausing gives us an ideal opportunity to look forward to our future destination, as well as to gaze backwards. We can be full of gratitude to God for the progress that we have already made, even as we check our compass bearings for the road ahead. And we can begin to recognize how our journey into growth has changed us so that we are no longer the same person who began the climb all those months and years ago. Yet we must resist the temptation inherent in these resting places to divert a little off the path, to find a particularly appealing contour to circle around rather than continuing to journey to the top.

Mountain walking

However life does not always feel as if we are hiking up a sharp steep hill. As any seasoned walker will tell you, the terrain on the way to the top of the mountain can be incredibly diverse. There are times when we can bounce happily through lush green meadows, marveling at God's bountiful grace. Yet there are also times when we limp wearily through drought-parched lands, desperate for just a tiny drop of refreshment from God's hands. The precise contours will be different for each one of us, however whether life feels like an uphill trudge or a pleasant amble by a stream, the path of growth continues to beckon us onwards and upwards so we might reach the point where our vision is utterly consumed by God.

Maybe this is where the language of mountain walking speaks to us most clearly, for just as ascending an incline requires continual effort and attention, so does the journey of our growth. Even when the path seems relatively easy and the way ahead is broad and smooth, we cannot afford to get complacent. We need to take care that our ankles are not twisted by loose and rugged stones, and that we stay alert to the relevant landmarks and signposts to keep us on God's track.

Worshiping God

Perhaps the greatest challenge is to remember that are here upon this earth to learn to worship God in every circumstance and to explore what it means to be in relationship with God. This is the very reason for our existence and the purpose of our growth. We are part of a story of such huge dimensions that our minds can scarcely take it in. By sending us to live upon this earth and physically cloaking us in our unique and intricate human forms, God has enabled us to appreciate our 'otherness' from him.

The distinction between us and God could not be greater: he is the Creator and we are the created; he is the Only Absolute whilst we are one of many relative beings he has created: as such we owe everything to him. And yet he has imprinted us with his divine likeness right through the details of our human form, to help us remember the heritage to which we have been born. Our identity flows out of the astonishing fact that we are his children as well as being the product of his hands, something that means we can relate to God, our Father, in the most intimate of terms. Even more amazingly, God has chosen to share our experience of physical separation from him by entering this world in human form. Through Jesus the purpose of our relative existence thus becomes complete, for by his death on the cross he has transcended the boundaries of our physicality and provided the way for us to meet with God.

The outward changes that we undergo are only part of the story, for alongside each physical outer change there is a much slower internal shift, or transition, as we move from one sense of identity to another.[2] The first step in this inner process is making an ending with the past. We cannot begin to embrace what is new while we remain entranced by the old, nor can we invest our time and energy in moving forward if it is still tied up in maintaining things as they have always been. Change is only possible when we are prepared to say goodbye. To use a gardening metaphor, we must dig up or cut down the plants that are no longer flourishing, and tear out all the thorny weeds and deep-rooted thistles to thoroughly prepare the ground for future growth.

Making endings

Growth is full of endings which come in their own way and in their own time, and every loss that we experience will create an ending of some kind. This loss is not always something physical; it may be something that impacts us in social, emotional or spiritual terms. Anything that moves us deeply is significant, and the intensity of our reaction to each loss will vary according to the exact circumstances, our previous experiences and our personality. Whether we are leaving the security of a long-term job or terminating a relationship that is pulling us away from God; moving away from a pleasant neighborhood or dealing with an unexpected shock; adjusting to a lack of freedom or discarding a favored item that no longer works, we must allow ourselves to grieve appropriately.

Every loss scenario holds within it some potential for growth, and with God's help our grieving can be transformed into a hopeful act in which we disentangle ourselves emotionally from the past so that we can enter into the promising future God has planned. As we will see in Chapters 3 and 4, this process begins as we learn to face up to the strong emotions that our losses evoke, and encounter the truth of God so that we can see where we need to change. In this way God enables us to remove the dead wood, tangled weeds and rubble, to clear the ground, so we can leave the past behind in a wholesome and healthy way.

The neutral zone

The next stage in an internal shift or transition is the neutral zone. This is an in-between phase, the psychological equivalent of a no man's land. The inner space that has been created by making endings with the past has not yet been filled, and so we swing from frothing with excited anticipation to feeling vulnerable, unsettled and unsafe. It is a time of great inner discomfort, restlessness and frustration, in which we are full of questions as we long both for the comfort and safety of the old way of life and for tangible signs that a new beginning is on its way.

The neutral zone or void is a stage where much courage and determination is needed to keep forging ahead, believing that the new beginnings God has promised will emerge when the time is right. As we wait, we must do the hard spade work of preparing the ground so that the conditions for germination and future growth are just right. We do this by listening to our inner questions and reflecting on life, by recognizing that we have a choice in how we will respond to life, and by harnessing the energy of our willingness and allowing God to work in and through the power of our intent. It is a process that takes much time and energy, as we go over and over the same clods of earth, carefully removing pernicious roots and stones, so that the soil can be broken down into a fine tilth.

Yet the neutral zone is not just about hard graft; it is also a place of opportunity and creativity, where we discover promising seedlings in the undergrowth and bring previously hidden plants into the light. Then, as the preparation work draws to a close, we sow our seeds expectantly, eagerly longing for the first tangible signs of new life.

New beginnings

The final part of a transition is the stage of new beginnings. The seeds planted in the neutral zone begin to unfurl and the plants start to put on fresh new growth. 'Like any organic process, beginnings cannot be made to happen by a word or action. They happen when the timing of the transition process allows them to happen, just as flowers and fruit appear on a schedule that is natural and not subject to anyone's will.'[3] We must learn to wait patiently for God's timing, no matter how difficult that may seem, for if we uproot the seeds of our ideas too early or fail to protect them properly, frosts or pests may damage the delicate new growth. Exploring new senses of identity will often leave us feeling vulnerable, and experimenting with new ways of being can make us feel exposed. Nevertheless, it is our responsibility to water the ground gently and uproot the weeds of our impatience and frustration so that in God's time the fledgling plants can produce beautiful blossom and go on to bear good fruit.

Growth and transitions

Life is made up of a multitude of transitions as we respond internally to an almost ceaseless amount of external change. Yet through it all God, the Unchanging One, is constantly wooing us and seeking to draw us to his side. He accompanies us through every external and internal change we make, and, whether we are dealing with an anticipated life event or adjusting to a sudden change of role, grieving for a friendship we have lost or relocating to another town, he is there by our side, inviting us to view things as he sees them, through the lenses of his love and grace. As we grasp the truth that we are held securely in his arms, he enables us to embrace our transitions wholeheartedly so they can become unique opportunities for further growth. Throughout this long and turbulent process God calls others to walk alongside, to encourage, challenge and inspire us as we seek to grow closer to him.

The journey of our growth runs right through our various transitions, as we use them to help us spiral ever onwards and upwards and deeper into ourselves and God. It is a cyclical journey that continually amazes and fascinates us as we seek to adventure on with God. Life on earth, complete with all its limitations, brokenness and pain, is the perfect setting for this process to take place. Our task is to accept the invitation God is holding out to us, to grow through our various transitions, and to see the challenges and opportunities of our endings, our neutral zones, and our new beginnings as opportunities to draw closer to him.

CHAPTER 2

THE IMPORTANCE OF GROWING

'Put your mind on your life with God. The way to life- to God!- is vigorous and requires your total attention.' (Luke 13.24, *The Message*)

It may seem obvious to state, but 'growing' is a verb. It is an action word that calls us forth, beckons us to travel on with God, and leave our well-worn comfort zones behind. It also implies forward movement, continual momentum, and a future waiting to unfurl. Contrast it to the noun 'growth', a word that has the action seemingly all tied up and in the past. It may be semantics, but those two or three letters make all the difference to our outlook, to how we choose to move through life. Do we see growth as an event that primarily happened in the past, a passive process that went on largely outside our conscious control? Or do we view growing as an ongoing and dynamic process, a 'doing' word, an evolving story in which we play an active part?

For most of us growing will not always proceed along a smooth and easy path. Life is more interesting and unpredictable than that. In the introduction I alluded to the significant role that Richard, my late husband, played in my own personal journey, and how the seeds of my passion for growing were sown during the time we shared. These seeds, pressed down and trampled upon for many years in the busyness of my life, did not begin to germinate and unfurl until the pain of grief could crack the hard soil of my heart.

As I look back now, I can see that God had been preparing the ground for many years before, through my upbringing in a Christian family and through my education. My faith journey, tentatively begun as a shy and retiring child, was cemented as I tearfully gave my heart to Jesus in my early teens after reading a book by Patricia St. John.[1]

Later, at University, my eyes were opened through meeting new friends to a way of relating to God as a loving Father who cared passionately for me. As I began to explore my faith in less formal terms, I was filled afresh with his Holy Spirit in a very tangible way.

Praying and reading my bible have played central roles in keeping me anchored to God through the years, as has regular church attendance, but there have been many times when this has been an uphill struggle. My understanding of God has shifted over the years from that of a well-respected and awesome Master I dare not displease, to that of a compassionate and ever loving Father and Heavenly King.

As I have journeyed along, I have experienced some significant growth spurts as God has opened my eyes to fresh understandings of his grace. However I have also experienced the discomfort of growing pains as I have grappled with deep questions in my heart and learned to come to terms with his sovereignty over my life. Through it all, I have become convinced that growing is a lifelong journey in which we can all engage. Each of us will come to it in our own individual way, yet the goal is always the same: to draw closer to God.

The Maker's design

Growing is a phenomenal concept, not least for the diversity of images that it brings to mind. Perhaps for you the word conjures up pictures of springtime, with newly planted seedlings bursting into life, fresh green shoots appearing on the trees and young lambs frolicking in the fields. Maybe you see images of boisterous, lively children, full of boundless energy and always increasing in size. Or you might find yourself looking back over your own journey of development, and recalling some of the joys and frustrations you experienced whilst growing up.

Growing is a fundamental pillar of life on earth, and an integral part of our Maker's design for us as individuals. From that first instant when we were conceived, when our father's sperm met our mother's egg, we were programmed to grow. First the cells divided and formed the primitive streak. From there the neural tube developed, and all the organs were set in place before we had even taken one breath of air outside our mother's womb. An exceptional amount of growing went on in this secret place as our tissues were created and the seeds of our future potential were sown. Once birth had occurred, our development continued in a more visible form, as our size enlarged and our actions came increasingly under our voluntary control. Gradually we were transformed by an amazing feat of God's engineering into a child, utilizing vast amounts of energy in the process. As puberty duly ensued, our bodies continued to change as we gradually took on our adult form, so that by the age of 20 to 25 the physical aspects of our development were, in all likelihood, complete.

However, our physical maturation was only a small part of our total growing. Throughout this time of immense bodily change, we were given the opportunity to develop a huge range of mental and social skills, as our circumstances and situations allowed. We began to separate ourselves from those around us as we assumed an individual identity of our own, and we attempted to become increasingly more independent from our primary care givers, with varying degrees of success. We learned to make decisions for ourselves without constant reference to authority figures, and we invested energy in creating our own social networks of friends. As the age of adulthood arrived, some of us even chose to leave home, as if to cement our status as a fully-fledged 'grown-up'.

These journeys into physical, social and mental maturation were, for the most part, simultaneous. Each aspect of our development informed and influenced the others in ways that were complex, mysterious and, at times, utterly confusing. It was not possible for us to cordon off the different areas of our lives and grant only some of them permission to grow, however hard we might have tried. This is because we were made as unified beings, constructed in an awesome way by an even more awesome God. Our physical, social and mental natures were designed to intersect and interact, and were intricately inter-woven for a purpose: to help us to fulfill our potential, and to work alongside each other in order that we might grow as a whole.

The spiritual nature

However, growing is not merely about attaining physical, social, or even mental independence from those who have given us care. It is far broader than this, and impacts us in a much deeper way. The bible tells us that our distinctiveness as human beings derives from our unique spiritual nature. We alone out of all the creatures of the earth are an extraordinary combination of heaven and earth. We have been physically molded from the earth and have received our life as a direct result of God's in-breathing (Gen. 2.7), an act that highlights our unique relationship with him.

Our spiritual nature is not confined to a distinct and discrete part of our body or brain, nor is it partitioned off from all the other segments of our lives. Rather it acts like a unifying thread, knitting together all the other strands into one cohesive whole, and bringing the physical, social and mental aspects of our being alive. It helps us to make sense of the bigger picture of our life, inviting us to see everything within the context of God's love; and it provides us with a purpose and a reason for our growth.

Growing is an inherently spiritual act, for it grants us the opportunity to further our relationship with God. It is a continual process with no age limit attached, for no matter how young we are or how old, there will always be more to learn and understand about ourselves and God.

Journeying towards God

Like any good relationship, our growing towards God will take much time. There are no short cuts or prizes for reaching the finishing post first, for it is not possible to measure a relationship in these terms. Nor is it possible to circumvent the journey without the risk of having to re-learn lessons all over again. Growing is a process that needs time to unfold so that each building block can be set down in its correct place, carefully resting on those that have gone before. We cannot afford to ignore the foundations of our growth, the truth of our identity in God, if the building of our life is to stand firm. Just as infancy needs to come before childhood, which must itself precede adult maturity, so too we must be careful how we build our lives spiritually if we are to continue to grow towards God.

This journeying is an active pursuit that requires us to invest energy and resources, as well as time. We are called to be as active as we are able in the journey of our growth, especially spiritually, for it simply will not happen by itself. There may be times when our growth appears to be disproportionately large compared to the meager amount of energy we have put in, when we are simply the recipients of God's amazing grace. For the most part, however, our growth into maturity is a slow and incremental process that requires much effort and time. It is a continually active journey of dialogue and engagement with God in the everyday situations of our lives; an on-going voyage of discovery and exploration as we allow our circumstances to teach us more about God and about ourselves, so that our lives may be brought more and more in line with God's ways.

Our growing is therefore a lively interface with the Divine, a constantly active adventure of trust, where we bring every aspect of our lives, physical, social, and mental, under the influence of God's grace. As we learn to repeatedly offer ourselves to God in response to the overwhelming love that he has shown to us through Jesus' death upon the cross, God invites us to embark upon a continuous process of submitting our lives to him, using the details of our daily lives to draw us on into an increasing awareness of our need of him. As we find ourselves responding to the magnitude of his love, God then uses our situations and our circumstances to mold us into the people he created us to become.

Growing and belonging

Growing draws us into a deep and fascinating exploration of what it means to belong to God, an adventure that engages us at all times and on all levels, if we allow it to do so. It is energizing and yet also demanding, captivating and yet freeing, challenging and yet full of grace and ease, disturbing and yet illuminating, and sometimes very hard work. Best of all, it brings us closer to God, the Author of Life himself, the one who initiated life in order that we might learn what it means to be in a relationship with him. As we learn to pursue this relationship of love, we are slowly transformed by the miracle of his grace, so that we gradually become more like him.

The path of growth leads right through the path of our individuality. As we are transformed by the power of his grace, we are enabled to take hold of the gift of our distinctiveness in a new way. We begin to realize the unique plans and purposes which we have been carefully designed by God to fulfill, and to accept the invitation God holds out to use our individuality for the glory of his name.

Responding to God's love

The path of our growth leads right through the territory of our heart to bring us back to God again and again. We are invited to look ever more deeply within in order that we might see where our lives have strayed from God's ways; to open the doors of our heart ever more widely so that he might fill us with his love and grace; and to allow God to transform us by his love and draw us on again. As we grasp the reality of his love within our inner parts, the external practicalities of our lives can then be brought more closely into line. In this way we help to bring God's kingdom here on earth.

Growing is not an intrinsically selfish act, where we seek to put our needs above those of the people who surround us, trampling on their lives to reach a higher plane of existence for ourselves. Rather, it is a self-giving response to the overwhelming love that we have received from God, through Jesus' death for us upon the cross. God's love is so huge and so immense that it cannot help but draw us on into an ever deepening relationship of love with him. As our love for him grows, he enables us to choose to put the needs of others before our own, as Jesus did, in order that others might journey with us into the warmth of God's embrace, and this in turn stimulates our own individual growth.

Preparing for eternity

Growing is a vital part of our preparation for eternity. Life here on earth is such a small part of our total existence. We have been made for so much more, and our hearts are meant to ache for that greater place where everything is renewed and restored and we can dwell with God for ever. Until that time, our task is to help each other to grow into the people God designed us to be before the world even began and fulfill our part in the next chapter of his story here on earth. We need to learn from the opportunities this life has to offer, and invest ourselves in things that are of eternal value, recognizing that our way back home involves an intimate and intricate journey through the range of experiences we now call life. We must view our existence in the light of eternity by looking beyond the temporal impermanent problems we now face, in order that we might become more fully the people God designed us to be.

We need to fix our vision on our eternal home, and realize that, by God's grace, a bigger story is beginning to unfurl even through the mundane aspects of our lives. Who we are being in the midst of our ceaseless activities is of vital significance. We must learn to lift our eyes off the petty annoyances and irritations of our current situations, and embrace the invitation God holds out, an invitation to journey towards him, to grow.

If we choose to ignore or decline this invitation, then our lives may become dreary and inert, unfulfilling and predictable. Comfort and safety have then become more important to us than our relationship with God, and we find ourselves stuck in a prison of our own making, with no obvious escape route. In a feeble attempt to avoid being shaken out of our status quo, we miss out on the larger picture of what God wants to do in our world, and fail to enter the dynamic challenge of being a partner in that work with him as we shy away from the exploration, learning, and adventure that he presents. In effect we tell God that this current existence is all we are living for, and our relationship with him is not worth bothering about. We are in danger of losing the very essence of life itself, as we fail to recognize our growing as a gracious invitation from the Lord. If we choose to accept this invitation, our lives will be filled with the fresh clean water of God's grace. As this refreshing water then courses through our hearts, it will begin to overflow to the world around, so that God can use us to take the good news of his love to those who are barren and dry.

Engaging with God

The process of our growth requires us to engage deeply with God through Jesus. The primary way of doing this is by allowing his Spirit to speak to us both through his Word, the bible, and in the context of prayer, for these are the greatest tools that he has given us to draw us into a deeper relationship with him.

Growing is thus far more than simply a program of study engaging only our mind. It is a heart process too that takes us ever deeper within as we grapple with God's truth and integrate it into our lives; an inner journey which expands our horizons, filling us with an air of expectancy and hope; a voyage of discovery that is charged with possibility and crosses many varied terrains as we explore new possibilities with God. In his letter to the Philippians, Paul writes: 'Not that I have already obtained all this, or have already been made perfect, but I press on to take hold of that for which Christ Jesus took hold of me. Brothers, I do not consider myself yet to have taken hold of it. But one thing I do: forgetting what is behind and straining towards what is ahead, I press on towards the goal to win the prize for which God has called me heavenwards in Christ Jesus' (Phil. 3.12-14). I believe that in Paul we have an example of someone who was continually growing. His divine encounter on the Damascus road left him in no doubt that it was God through Jesus that he should pursue. From then on he was constantly striving towards his heavenly goal, no matter how harsh his physical circumstances, seeing them merely as opportunities for God to be at work in and through him.

In the same way our growing is a constant journey of re-evaluation in the light of God's enormous love, and an active partnership with God within the minute details of our lives. It is a process of dethroning self in favor of God's Lordship in our lives, an invitation to see his greater purposes at work, and a personal voyage heavenwards, even as heaven seeks to reign right now within our hearts.

Being ourselves

Growing is an individual journey which we are all invited to undergo in our own way and at our own pace. God does not ride roughshod over the details of our lives, asking us all to conform to one particular mold. Instead he has given us our own distinctive personalities and experiences in order that they might be used to draw us closer to him.

Learning to be ourselves is the journey of a lifetime. It is a task we cannot delegate. God invites us to concentrate our efforts on being the person he created us to be, for he does not want us to be anyone else. God is constantly wooing us, initiating and sustaining the whole process of our growing, in order that we might become more fully the people he created us to be. And so that we might know his heart is constantly for us, even when we make mistakes, he has willingly given his Son, Jesus, to die in our place and rise again in order that we might be forgiven and set free.

Our growing is therefore the ongoing work of God's salvation within us, reclaiming the captured territories of our lives as we learn to live in an attitude of continual dependence on him. It is a process that requires us to take responsibility for ourselves and to make some fundamental choices about how we will live our life, subjects which we will cover more fully in Chapters 7 and 9.

Building blocks

The journey of growing is unique for each one of us, and yet it seems as if there are some common building blocks that can help us all to grow. These are: acknowledging how we feel, encountering the truth of God, learning to reflect on life, understanding the role of relationships, choosing wisely, utilizing the energy of our willingness and allowing God to work through the power of our intent, taking responsibility for ourselves and for our growth, and aligning ourselves with God's perfect plans. The remainder of this book will provide a detailed consideration of each of these building blocks, along with a final chapter looking at how we can help each other to grow.

CHAPTER 3

ACKNOWLEDGING OUR EMOTIONS

'You made all the delicate, inner parts of my body and knit me together in my mother's womb. Thank you for making me so wonderfully complex! Your workmanship is marvellous- how well I know it.' (Ps. 139:13-14, New Living Translation)

Our emotions are good and generous gifts from a good and generous God who longs for us to grow. We need to embrace them as welcome signposts in our lives for they reveal much about the world that lies beneath.

Learning to acknowledge our emotions is a risky business; in all likelihood it will lead us to experience a much broader range of feelings than we have experienced before. We may be fortunate enough to receive foretastes of the heavenly realm, with sublime moments of inexpressible joy and peace as we sense our deep connectedness with God. However we may also feel deeper anguish and sharper pain as we look upon this broken, fallen world and face up to our own duplicity and sin.

In this chapter we will look at our inherent capacity to feel, and how this reflects something of our unique likeness to God. We will then explore the importance of acknowledging our emotions and using them as tools to help us journey into growth.

Journeying into acceptance

The journey into learning to accept my emotions has been a lengthy one for me. As a child I quickly learnt that showing my emotions, particularly the more negatively perceived ones, set off emotional responses in those around. Those responses, although not severe in any way, unsettled me nevertheless as I felt responsible for what I had done, and helpless in the face of them. My erroneous conclusion was that emotions were dangerous and wrong, and so I did my best to hide them under layers of pretending to be okay. I buried myself in books and solitary pursuits, and wore a mask all the time, in an attempt to curtail their unwanted activity. The result was that over the years I became more and more distant from myself. I lost touch with my feelings almost completely, and was therefore forced to rely on the subjective opinions of those around. It seemed easier to hide behind other people and their preferences rather than risk opening up my own Pandora's Box of emotions.

It took a brave man, Richard, to ask me to be his wife when I was in my early twenties. He saw through my carefully erected defenses, and, with God's help, I was finally able to let the mask down. The emptiness behind was utterly enormous, as years of emotional neglect had left their mark. I struggled to get in touch with the emotions that I had buried for so long, and found it hard to accept that my own shaky opinions were worthwhile.

As I regained lost ground and allowed my emotions to surface once again, I became aware that they were far more important than I had previously realized. The diverse feelings that were now coursing through me day by day were the raw materials that made up my life. By observing my reactions to the circumstances I found myself in, and to previous events, I found that I was able to learn more about myself. In addition, I also discovered more about my relationship with God. I began to see that God had made me in his image, to be like him in some small way, and as I poured out my barrage of emotions to him, it seemed that he was using them to draw me to his side. Just as I spoke of my feelings when I shared my life with my husband, Richard, so I could bring my emotions to God, knowing that he could hold them safely in his hands and use them in his way. God had created my emotions, he knew intimately what I was like, and, despite all, he still loved me.

Understanding ourselves

Over time I have come to see that God longs for all his children to open up their emotions to him. The image of an adult trying to elicit feelings from a child comes to mind, knowing that the end result will not only afford them a greater understanding of the child's perception of events, but will also aid the child's understanding of themselves. Of course our Heavenly Father already knows exactly how we feel, for nothing is ever hidden from him. Yet even so he wants us to tell him about our emotional reactions to life, in order that we might understand ourselves better and grow towards him.

Acknowledging our emotions is an integral part of growing into life. When we recognize our emotions we can then begin to decode the messages they bring, messages alerting us to the areas where we are unconsciously hurting ourselves, others, and God, and messages about where our relationship with God is less than it could be. In addition, as we forge deeper connections within our lives between our innermost thoughts and our outward behaviors, we gain a deeper understanding of who we are as unique individuals, and of the amazing love that God has shown towards us.

We are all fallen creatures, and it is wise to remember that our emotions may lead us astray, especially if we idolize them. However, we must also bear in mind that our emotions are God-given tools. They are there to enrich our lives as well as to identify the deep sources of pain that have lain buried and forgotten for years. They are an integral part of our likeness to God, helping us to reflect his image in the world even whilst they reveal to us where we have become estranged from his ways. It is only as we learn to acknowledge and express our emotions that we can grow to be more fully the people that God designed us to be.

Made to feel

All of us are made to feel. From the moment we awaken in the morning to the minute we fall asleep, our lives are full of our subjective responses to the world around. Whether we consider feelings in terms of touching and making physical contact, or in terms of the spontaneous perceptions and impressions that arise inside our minds, their purpose seems to be the same: to enable us to make sense of life and experience it in our own unique way.

Each external stimulus comes with the potential to provoke a distinctive and personal internal reaction, a response which may affect us both physically and emotionally. Occurring from the moment of our birth and almost certainly well before, every situation and every circumstance we encounter can leave an impression on our body and our mind. This means that over time layers upon layers of experience are gradually built up as we develop and continue to respond to the individual nuances of our life, at least partly on the basis of what has gone before.

Made in the image of God

Our emotions, just like feelings in their broadest sense, are a fundamental aspect of our human form. They help us to perceive life in our own individual way, and grant us an incredible and unique sensitivity to the world in which we live. The sheer diversity of our emotions is part of the gift for us. Life would be extremely dull without them. Sorrow and pain would not be counterbalanced by joy and peace, grief and anger by laughter and gratitude. God has given us such a wide range of emotions to share with others and with him. We can laugh with him, cry with him, tell him our heartache and pain; we can experience true happiness and contentment, and know the inner joy and peace that only he can bring. Emotions are there to enrich our lives, to enhance our experience whilst we dwell upon this earth, to make our lives fuller and more complete. 'Our emotions were given not to control us, but that we might be able to enjoy life.'[1]

Emotions are not limited to a chosen few, or restricted to an isolated part of the world. Wherever we live, and whatever our origins, we will all experience emotions. Nor are emotions something we must work hard to acquire or aspire to attain. The fact that facial expressions of emotion are remarkably similar worldwide, even between very diverse cultures, indicates an underlying and universal genetic cause.[2] Emotions are an integral part of the Maker's design, coming as gracious and generous gifts from our Creator, God, given to us freely and without reserve. They are an essential aspect of our humanness and reveal something of our likeness to God.

The opening chapter of the bible makes it very clear that humans are made in the image of God, something that sets us apart from all the other creatures of the earth. 'Let us create man in our image, in our likeness', God declares on the sixth day of creation (Gen. 1.26), an action that is so important that the narrative reiterates it with the words: 'God created man in his own image, in the image of God he created him' (Gen. 1.27). Each of us is designed to reflect something of God's nature to the world, and our emotional capacity is an intrinsic part of this. Our distinctiveness as human beings is not limited to our physical appearance; it also encompasses the non-physical, intangible aspects of our lives, including our emotions. How we respond to life and how we feel is part of our incredible uniqueness, and through it we are able to express something of our privileged resemblance to God.

God's emotions

The bible is littered with expressions of God's emotions, both explicit and implicit. In the Old Testament we witness God's *satisfaction* as he creates the world, declaring that the earth he has made is good (Gen. 1.10). Later we learn that God is *pleased* with Noah, in contrast with all the other people of his day, because Noah chooses to walk with God, an emotion that leads God to give Noah detailed instructions to build an ark in order that he and his family might survive the catastrophic flood that God brings on the earth (Gen. 6.8). In Exodus we hear of God's *compassion* for his people as they are cruelly enslaved by the Egyptians, something that causes him to ask Moses to speak to the Egyptian king on their behalf and ultimately lead them into freedom (Ex. 3.7-10). In Deuteronomy we learn of God's feelings of *delight* when the Israelites turn to him with all their heart and all their soul (Deut. 30:9). And in the book of 1 Kings we are told that God feels *pleasure* when the young King Solomon asks for wisdom at the start of his reign, rather than petitioning God for worldly wealth or fame (1 Kgs 3.10).

The Old Testament also gives us examples of God feeling less agreeable emotions. His heart is filled with *grief* and *pain* when he sees how wicked mankind has become, and this prompts him to flood the earth yet rescue Noah so that life on earth can start again (Gen. 6.6). Later we hear of his *disappointment* when the Israelites are so eager to be like the surrounding nations that they request a human king, effectively rejecting him as their sovereign (1 Sam. 8.7). We also observe God's *sadness* when the first king to be chosen, Saul, deliberately disobeys his instructions and fails to destroy everything belonging to his enemies (1 Sam. 15.11). And we hear of God's *displeasure* when the second king, David, commits adultery and follows it with murder in a futile attempt to hide what he has done (2 Sam. 11.27).

In the New Testament, God's emotions are again expressed. God the Father audibly declares his undiluted *pleasure* with his Son, Jesus, on the occasion of his baptism in the River Jordan (Matt. 3.17), a sentiment which is later reiterated when Jesus goes up a mountain and takes on a heavenly appearance in front of Peter, James and John (Matt.17.5). In the Gospels we also observe God the Son, Jesus, experiencing emotions in a fully human way. We hear Jesus expressing *surprise* as his mother looks to him to sort out the dwindling refreshment supply at a wedding in Cana

(John 2.4), and we see his deep *distress* at the Pharisee's stubbornness to believe he is the Messiah when he heals a man on the sabbath day (Mark 3.5). We note Jesus' *amazement* at the faith of a Roman Centurion who believes that Jesus can heal his servant simply by speaking the word (Luke 7.9), and we watch him weeping openly as an expression of his *grief* when he is told that his good friend Lazarus has died (John 11.35). We look on as Jesus' *anger* explodes in the temple forecourts, turning over the tables of the money changers in protest at the way that his Father's house has become a den of thieves (Mark 11.15-17), and we witness his intense *anguish* in the garden of Gethsemane as he commits himself to following his Father's will (Luke 22.44). Finally we listen as he expresses feelings of *abandonment* as he is left alone on the cross to die (Matt. 27.46).

Not a mistake

Our emotions are not a mistake. They are an integral part of our human design, a crucial aspect of our similarity to God. We have been made in God's image (Gen. 1.4-5), and so it is hardly surprising that we experience the same emotions as he does. God does not expect us to go through anything that he himself is not prepared to undergo. He understands firsthand the way our human emotions can affect us and the reactions that they can trigger in our lives. He has felt the inner turbulence and upheaval they can create. Through Jesus God has identified himself fully with us, and through our emotions he invites us to share in his divine life (Heb. 2.17).

The biblical narrative is packed with examples of people showing their emotions. Take the story of Jacob, for example, and the *fear* and *dread* he experiences as he prepares to be reunited with his twin brother Esau many years after an unresolved family feud (Gen. 32.7). Or think of Joseph, *overcome with emotion* as he finally sees his blood brother Benjamin again after a long and difficult separation (Gen. 43.30). Consider Moses' burning *anger* when he sees God's people dancing before a golden calf rather than worshiping the Lord (Ex. 32.19), and contrast it to the people's shouts of *joy* when they see the glory of the Lord for themselves as Aaron is consecrated as High Priest (Lev. 9.24). Observe childless Hannah as she pours out her heart, desperately *yearning* to hold a baby of her own (1 Sam. 1.11). Or remember David dancing with *delight* as the ark of the covenant, the special symbol of God's presence, is brought up to the capital city of Jerusalem (2 Sam. 6.14). Each of these in their own way offers us some insight into the character of God, some glimpse of the depth and variety of emotions that he feels.

An integral part of the whole

The book of the bible that is perhaps most associated with emotional outpourings is the book of Psalms. In this collection of private and corporate songs and prayers we find an amazing variety of raw and undiluted emotions described in remarkably candid terms. Read through Psalm 6 as a starting point, and you will soon realize that no emotion is too awful or exhilarating to serve as an opportunity to draw close to God.

Yet despite the fact that many emotions are clearly displayed throughout the books of the bible, it is very difficult to find specific teaching or references in scripture to the actual word 'emotion'. This is because in biblical terms it is simply not possible to separate our emotional capacity from the rest of our being. The bible tells us that we are created as one whole, a remarkable fusion of physical matter and divine breath, exquisitely and intimately intertwined. There is no clear defining line. We cannot be neatly divided into separate parts. Our emotions are an integral part of the whole and can arise from and affect all parts of our body at one and the same time.[3]

In the scriptures, therefore, words for physical body parts are used to describe and represent the emotional state of the whole. We hear of bones being out of joint and hearts turning to wax (Ps.

22.14), bowels churning (Job 30.27), and distressing torment felt deep within (Lam. 1.20), hearts being broken and bones trembling (Jer. 23.9), and 'war within [my] members' (Rom. 7:23). Whether the word for heart, bowels, kidneys, insides or the mind is employed, it is emphasizing the same truth: our emotions are an integral part of the whole. Many of the nuances have been lost in the English translations, perhaps helpfully at times as over 80 different words for body parts are used in the original Hebrew and Greek.[4] Nevertheless it is still possible to pick up the overall theme: each of us has been created as a unified entity, one cohesive whole, and our emotions are an intrinsic part of this. Thus instructions on trusting God with all our heart (Prov. 3.5-6), and guarding our heart as the wellspring of life (Prov. 4.23), serve as reminders of the complexity of our intrinsic design, and call us into a greater awareness of the holistic nature of our lives.

Understanding our emotions

Each of us has a unique life story to tell, and no two lives are ever exactly the same. The individual conditions we have encountered and the distinctive situations we have come up against have all played their part in shaping who we are today. It is these same circumstances that have helped to determine the exact emotions we experience and how we choose to behave.

Rather than being given simple feedback loops that always elicit the same response, we have been endowed with intricate and complicated emotional machinery which enables us to react to life in a multitude of different ways. Our emotions are often based upon past happenings, the details of which have long been forgotten, and this, coupled with the fact that they largely arise spontaneously, outside of our conscious control, means that they can, at times, be extremely difficult to understand.

The huge variety of emotions possible, along with the enormous variation in intensity, also gives rise to further confusion. We are capable of such diverse feelings. From the deepest groans of pain to the most sublime ecstasies of joy, through the numbing effects of freshly entered grief to the excitement of longed for anticipation, and from the debilitating effects of acute anxiety and fear to the lightness and exhilaration of spontaneous laughter, the range is seemingly too vast for words.

Yet our emotions have not been designed simply to confound us and leave us feeling puzzled; instead it seems that this vast array of possible emotions exists to fulfill a specific purpose within our lives: to serve as a bridge between the physical and non-physical dimensions of our lives and point us towards the one who made them, God. They showcase the magnificence of his infinite creative talent in a way that nothing else can, as he blends and mixes our assorted emotions within the details of our lives. Moreover these same emotions, variable and varied as they are, provide us with the opportunity to grapple with what it means to be like him.

Negative emotions

It is tempting at times to regard feelings as an unwanted appendage to our lives, particularly the emotions that we do not want to handle like anger, pain, rejection, frustration and grief. Some people even think of them as working against us, pushing us off course, and stilting our spiritual development. These people focus on the joy spoken of in the bible, and claim that happiness should be present at all times. Yet the bible contains many examples of God expressing these so-called negative emotions himself. He lets us know in no uncertain terms that he is a *jealous* God, that his *anger* is aroused when we seek to put other idols in his place (Deut. 5.8, 6.15), and that he feels *grief* and *displeasure* when his laws are broken time and time again (Gen. 6.6, Num. 32.10-13, 2 Kgs 22.13, Is. 63.10, Mal. 1.10). If God who is perfect allows himself to demonstrate emotions such as these, then perhaps we can permit ourselves to acknowledge them and communicate them carefully too.

Throughout the scriptures, and particularly in the New Testament, there is a strong and recurring theme: suffering now and glory later on.[5] We are told over and over again that this life is meant to be a testing place, full of troubles and trying circumstances (for example, John 16.33, Acts 14.22, 2 Cor. 4.17). Life is not meant to be always bathed in a rosy glow and provide us only with pleasurable experiences. Rather we are encouraged to hold unswervingly to the hope that we profess of the future glory that will one day be ours, even as we learn to patiently endure (Rom. 8.24-25, Rom. 12.2, James 5.7-8, Rev. 3.10). Our 'negative' emotions should therefore come as no surprise. They serve simply to remind us to continue to press on towards our heavenly goal, to journey onwards into growth.

The dangers of repressed emotions

There is now plenty of scientific evidence that expressing our emotions, including the so-called 'negative' emotions of anger, fear and sadness, is an intrinsically healthy act. It allows the chemicals that mediate emotions to flow freely around the body and integrate the response. In contrast, when we fail to convey our emotions for any length of time, the result is 'a massive disturbance of the body-mind network' which weakens the unity of the whole and may result in disease.[6]

Many counselors, psychotherapists, pastors and doctors can testify to the detrimental impact of unexpressed emotion in the lives of those they work with, both in terms of mental and physical dis-ease. It was Sigmund Freud who first described depression as being anger turned inwards and redirected at oneself. Perhaps depression is not the only condition that might arise if we fail to acknowledge how we feel. 'Our negative emotions such as bitterness, rejection, and anger, are not to be ignored. Just as bodily pain is God's way of telling us that something has gone awry with our physical nature, so emotional pain may tell us that all is not well with our spiritual nature.'[7]

Instead, it seems that often we prefer to run the other way. We bottle up our anxieties, hoping they will go away of their own accord; we refuse to admit our pain, because to acknowledge it would be to risk sinking without trace; and we fight the feelings of sadness and loss, worrying that if we allow them to have a voice they might consume us or overwhelm us with the blackness of despair. The result is that we recoil and back off, reducing the range of emotions we allow ourselves to embrace. We attempt to organize our lives in such a way as to ensure that we are not exposed to emotional pain. We take the comfortable route instead of the one that causes our heart to race, and we neuter our existence to insulate ourselves against feeling rejection and fear. We reduce our palate of feelings, and acquire a taste for the experiences we know will bring us a sense of security and superficial happiness. We seek to reject the tools that will refine us and help us grow, and accept only the ones that offer little challenge to the status quo. Our emotional capacity thus becomes diminished as we fail to remember that our diverse emotions are an inherent part of our God-given design, and we simply live in self-deceit as we try to ignore them.

Moreover, when we disallow our emotions and seek to repress or reject them in some way, we are on the slippery slope of disrespecting God. We are basically declaring that we do not like what he has made. We show that we are 'unprepared to do what God himself does'[8], and so we cut ourselves off from him, both by how we reflect his image, and in how we are able to relate directly to him.

Acknowledging our emotions

Learning to acknowledge our negative emotions can be quite a scary prospect. Ultimately the safest place for any of our emotions to be acknowledged is within the context of our relationship with God, for there we can know ourselves to be held securely in the warmth of his unconditional embrace. As we bring him our emotions, even in their rawest state, we open up the doors of dialogue between ourselves and God, and allow him to draw us into a deeper understanding of his love and grace.

The ways of acknowledging our emotions within this divine relationship are numerous and diverse, and many creative approaches can be used. The psalms can often provide a useful starting point in enabling us to articulate exactly how we feel. By echoing the psalmist's words, our own emotions are drawn out and turned God-wards in a context that is good and prayerful. Listening to music or writing in a journal can also help to unlock pent up emotions, as can talking honestly with a trusted confidant or friend. At other times we may need to create a picture or an object with our hands or go for a solitary walk in the countryside. The possibilities are almost endless and different approaches may be used at different times. What is important, however, is that we find a way of acknowledging our emotions to God so that we do not implode and cause damage to ourselves, or explode and cause injury to others.

Tools for growth

'Emotional wholeness cannot be achieved through denying the deep emotions that we all have from time to time.'[9] Yet no matter how potent our emotions may be, we must take care not to idolize them. Our emotions were never intended to be worshiped as gods in their own right. They are simply tools to equip us to grow towards God. Our emotions are always less important than God himself, and should never be given a higher priority in our lives than listening directly to him. Our relationship with God is fundamental. He alone is the One who is worthy to be worshiped, and he alone deserves to be number one in our lives. Emotions are merely instruments of our growth, to be used as tools as we seek to become more like him.

This is where God's ways depart markedly from those of the world. Instead of encouraging us to use temporary fixes to medicate our internal pains and frustrations away, God asks us to acknowledge how we feel (Phil. 4.6, 1 Peter 5.7) for he knows that only then will we be free to move on as he leads. Rather than relying on prescribed and non-prescribed substances and activities to alleviate our inner turmoil and distress, God calls us to listen to our emotions as warning signals, alerting us to what is going on underneath.

Decoding our emotions and interpreting them as pointers towards growth takes time and commitment, however we need to remember that we are not asked to do it alone. God is our constant guide and companion, and if we ask him for assistance, he will provide the support and encouragement we need to evaluate our emotions appropriately.

To summarize, our emotions, both negative and positive, display something of our innate likeness to God. They are good and generous gifts designed to enrich our lives and allow us to respond to life in our own unique way. As we learn to acknowledge the varying emotions that we feel both to ourselves and to God, we are drawn into a deeper understanding of ourselves and our relationship to him. In this context our emotions can then serve as vital tools to aid us in the journey of our growth.

CHAPTER 4

ENCOUNTERING THE TRUTH

'If you hold to my teaching, you really are my disciples. Then you will know the truth and the truth will set you free.' (John 8.32)

The fundamental truth of our existence is that we are loved by God. Learning to accept this glorious reality for ourselves gives us the courage we need to recognize where we still need to change. In this chapter we will look at what it means to come into a deeper encounter with the truth of our identity in God, and how that encounter can enable us to become more fully the people that he designed us to be.

Truth and light

'God is light. In him there is no darkness at all. If we claim to have fellowship with him yet walk in the darkness, we lie and do not live by the truth' (1 John 1.5-6). Not only do we need to live in the light of our varying emotions, as we saw in the last chapter, but we also need to live in the light of scriptural truth which is timeless and unchanging. We must allow the light of God's truths to transform our hearts and minds as the Holy Spirit leads us ever onwards toward God, so that we can evaluate our emotions accurately. As the Contemporary English Version puts it: 'Don't be like the people of this world, but let God change the way you think. Then you will know how to do everything that is good and pleasing to him' (Rom. 12.2). Pleasing God should be our central aim. This is the journey of our growth – learning to live a life that delights him in every detail, not because he demands it of us as a merciless overlord might do, but because his love compels us to respond in love to him. Our relationship with Jesus, the one who is The Truth, changes us from the inside out, renewing our minds and transforming our hearts bit by bit as he helps us to recognize where we need to change so we might become more like him (Rom. 8.29).

It is a process of gradual enlightenment as God shines the light of his truth into our lives. 'Whoever lives by the truth comes into the light, so that it may be seen plainly that what he has done has been done through God' (John 3.21). His truth acts like a search beam as it sweeps across our lives, exposing the parts we have kept hidden for some time, the dank, dingy areas that we have often shied away from, and the dark, dusty corners full of cobwebs that are long overdue for a spring clean (Prov. 20.27). God knows exactly how much light is needed to expose the cracks so he might heal them, and he knows how frail we really are. Lovingly he reveals his truth to us in stages, because otherwise it would be too much for us to bear. Our progress therefore comes in little increments as God enables us to absorb his truths into our lives and as we learn to recognize where we are hiding from his light.

Facing up to ourselves

Coming face to face with the truth of who we are is both exciting and unpleasant: exciting because it ultimately leads to greater freedom as we grasp the truth of our identity in God; unpleasant because it reveals our inherent sinfulness and the destructive behavior patterns that have become deeply ingrained.

If our desire is to grow into the people God intends us to be, then we must come to God in an attitude of openness and wait expectantly for him to reveal the truths that we need to hear. We do this safe in the knowledge that his timing is perfect and he knows exactly what we can bear. As we saw in the last chapter when we looked at the subject of emotions, God is interested in every aspect of our life. He does not want us to simply ignore our failings and limitations, for 'the grandest kind of perfection of who we are includes being honest about our dark sides, our imperfections. We find comfort when we know who someone else is, and it is just as important that we learn the truth about ourselves, the truth about who we are.'[1] For this reason we are invited to submit ourselves to the bright light of his transforming truth so that it can burn all our deficiencies and shortcomings away.

My business

I have already shared something of my own personal and rather painful journey. My encounter with the truth of who I am has often seen me writhing in agony, for as I have journeyed on with God, I have increasingly recognized how much I still need to change. I have become more acutely aware of the brokenness in my life and the places where I feel irretrievably stuck, and I know with utter certainty that if it were not for God's grace I could not continue to journey on. Yet even as I have grappled with my pain and frustration, I have become more and more convinced that, despite my frailty and my failures, God's love for me remains intact. His desire is that I become more like him in every way, using the raw materials of my current temporary physical existence to aid my learning and my growth. Nevertheless I still find it very easy to miss opportunities to learn vital lessons, and often seem to find myself blaming my circumstances or other people for how I feel. At those times I need to go back to God to ask for his forgiveness and for his help to find his truth again, and to see where it is that I, not others, need to change.

One of my favorite prayers is the 'Serenity prayer.'[2] It goes like this:

God,
Grant me
Serenity to accept the things I cannot change,
Courage to change the things I can, and

Wisdom to know the difference.

'The wisdom to know the difference' is something I struggle with on a regular basis. The truth is that there are many situations over which I have no control. It is not my place to tell God how he should run the universe day after day. That is up to him alone to decide. Nor can I have the audacity to flick out the specks of dust from the eyes of others whilst my vision is terribly impaired (Matt. 7.5, Luke 6.42). It seems that when I expect others to do the changing, I diminish the opportunity I then have for growth. When I stay in my business, accepting that there are some things in the world that I cannot change becomes easier, and my energy can be channeled more appropriately into noting where I myself need to change. In this way I can concentrate more fully on being the person God designed me to be and acting with integrity, compassion and truth, rather than getting bogged down in trying to run the lives of other people, or, worse still, attempting to play the role of God.

Byron Katie has put it so well: 'To think that I know what's best for anyone else is to be out of my business. Even in the name of love, it is pure arrogance, and the result is tension, anxiety and fear. Do I know what's right for myself? That's my only business. Let me work on that before I try to solve your problems for you.'[3]

The essence of our being

When God created Adam in his image in the Garden of Eden, he began by molding a body out of the dust of the earth. He then 'breathed into his nostrils the breath of life, and the man became a living being' (Gen. 2:7). In this way the spiritual and material aspects of life became inextricably intertwined. An organic union was forged between the two so that they became inseparable, and the physical nature became the means through which the spiritual or ontological nature could be expressed.

Like Adam, each of us has been given a body filled with

marvelous and intricate machinery, a complex and brilliant physical structure that was designed to perform thousands of compound tasks at one and the same time. Yet contained within this physical frame is something even more magnificent and beautiful: the essence of our being, our spiritual or ontological nature. The differences between these two aspects are marked. Whereas the physical self is solid, ephemeral, limited and finite, our spiritual nature is elusive, ethereal, immeasurable and without any tangible boundaries. Moreover, whilst our physical frame changes continually with the passing years, our spiritual or ontological nature remains essentially the same, imbuing us with a profound sense of dignity, worth and purpose as we journey towards God.

Identity and truth

Our identity is far greater than the physical body in which we temporarily reside, and even the most turbulent of our emotions cannot alter who we are. Life on earth as we know it now is only transitory, and we were made for so much more. One day we will be with God forever, and the whole of his creation will be completely renewed and restored. Our relationship with God is the constant thread that draws us on.

This theme is picked up in the book of Exodus where we meet God's people wandering restlessly in the wilderness as they learn and relearn the truth of their relationship with God. After forty years they are finally secure enough in their God-given identity to subdue the surrounding peoples and enter into Canaan, the land promised by God to be their permanent home.

Like the Israelites, we too are on a journey to our long-term home, a journey that flows from and is sustained by our relationship with God as we learn and relearn the truth of our identity and our relatedness to him. It is a journey that calls us to search diligently for the truth, no matter how difficult or incon-venient it may seem. We must be like a man who finds treasure hidden in a field and then sells everything to purchase that field (Matt. 13.44-46). We should 'buy the truth' and not sell it, as well as seeking 'wisdom, discipline and understanding' (Prov. 23.23), for truth, like wisdom and understanding, is of infinite value because it ultimately comes from God (Prov. 2.3-6).

We find this truth primarily by reading the scriptures for they are the inspired word of God. Teachers, traditions, fellow travellers and books can enlarge our understanding and show us where to look. God's truth is also embedded within creation, for 'truth flows from the earth' as Jean Vanier puts it, and this includes the 'earth' of our own bodies.[4] Thus there is also a sense in which truth can be worked out from within. 'When we begin to listen to our bodies, we begin to listen to reality through our own experiences' and so we move 'from theories we have learned to listening to the reality that is in and around us.'[5] Our search for truth is therefore not just a cerebral or intellectual matter; it is a search that involves the whole of us including our emotions and our heart.

The whole of our being, both physical and non-physical, has been made by God in his image, to resonate to the heartbeat of his love. Our current experience of humanity, with all its finite limitations and tangible boundaries, is the perfect forum for us to explore our relationship with God. This is the truth that we are searching for, the reality of who we are in relationship to God. Our search for truth invites us to acknowledge the greater-than-physical reality of our existence and recognize that our entire nature is designed to help us relate to God.

Reality and truth

The word 'truth' conveys a sense of honesty and integrity, of something verifiable that accurately conforms to a given standard and is 'in accordance with fact or reality, genuine, not spurious or counterfeit,'[6] 'imagined or made up.'[7] As such, truth is not a concrete object that we can physically possess. Rather, it is an unfolding understanding of the mystery of reality, for at its most fundamental the truth is simply what actually exists.

The reality which underpins all our human experiences is that we belong to God. It is a truth to which we must return over and over again, allowing it to sink ever deeper into our hearts and minds. Our identity is a direct result of God's immense and lavish grace and generosity to us, his children. Our relationship with him is bathed in such an enormous outpouring of his unconditional love that we can scarcely take it in. God loves us so passionately and so intensely that he was even prepared to choose to limit himself within the impermanent physical creation that he had made, to willingly share our fragile experience of humanity, and to deal with the consequences of our sin by dying a humiliating and excruciating death at the hands of those he had made.

We are loved purely because of who we are; we cannot earn God's love in any way. It is a truth that we must search out for ourselves, looking ever deeper into the recesses of our heart to find God waiting for us there. This truth, this reality, impacts every area of our lives as God invites us to explore the magnificence of who we are in him and it allows our being then to overflow in acts of gratitude and love.

The ultimate truth

God's immense love for us is the ultimate truth, the supreme reality of our lives. It is the filter through which everything else must be seen if we are to perceive our circumstances correctly. Thus pains and trials are not to be viewed as cruel punishments sent to penalize us for our wrongs, as sticks to beat us to make us good; rather they are challenges to sharpen us and draw us on into deeper experiences of trust and dependence on him. Likewise, tribulations and discouragements are not imposed on us by an angry God wanting to make us pay the full price for all our mistakes; instead they may be seen as golden opportunities to draw closer to him as he allows them in our lives (James 1.2-4, 2 Cor. 4.16-18). Even when we are left with unpleasant consequences as a result of destructive behavior patterns and foolish choices that we may have made, then we can still see God's hand at work, redeeming our mistakes for his glory and revealing more of his love and grace.

The truth of God's love for us is something we can forget all too easily as we seek to ignore his imprint on our lives. We act as if our wants and needs were paramount and push his loving overtures aside, and we let our negative emotions take precedence over the glorious truths we know in our heads. Yet no matter how much we try to neglect God or seek to mar his image in our lives, we cannot alter the truth that he is our Source and Creator, and our very being, both physical and non-physical, derives from our relationship to him.

Truth personified

Truth is not simply an abstract concept; it is dynamic and relational, and its fullest expression is found within the person of Jesus. John's Gospel in particular picks up this theme, clearly indicating in the first chapter that the completeness of God's truth is found only within Jesus (John 1.14, 17). From the very start of his public ministry, Jesus' words begin to ring out: 'I tell you the truth....' He repeats this phrase over and over again when he is teaching, to invite his listeners to recognize his divine authority to speak the truth.

John the Baptist openly witnesses to this, as does the Old Testament (John 5. 31, 39). However by far the weightiest testimony comes from God the Father, for, as Jesus says, 'the very work that the Father has given me to finish, and which I am doing, testifies that the Father has sent me' (John 5.36). 'If you hold to my teaching, you really are my disciples,' Jesus announces later to those who want to follow him, continuing: 'then you will know the truth and the truth will set you free'

(John 8.32). 'I am the way, the truth and the life,', he tells his floundering disciples as they still fail to understand why he has come (John 14.6). 'For this I came into the world,' he informs a bemused Pilate near the end of his earthly life, 'to testify to the truth. Everyone on the side of truth listens to me' (John 18:37). Jesus is truth personified. He is the greatest expression of truth that we can ever know.

God's enabling

Ultimately our search for the truth must lead us into a deep and personal encounter with the one who is The Truth, Jesus. The reality of his love can then begin to set us free from the sins that so easily entangle us and enable us to become the people that God designed us to be (John 8.32). We need to move beyond Pilate's question of 'What is truth?' to ask instead 'Who is truth?' so that our eyes can be opened to see the answer as he stands in front of us (John 18:38). It is an encounter that involves both our head and our heart as we spend time getting to know the person of Jesus through bible reading and through prayer. As we allow him to reveal himself to us and envelop us in his strong love, we can then begin to perceive reality correctly, as if through God's eyes.

Yet even as we attempt to discover more of the truth as found in Jesus, we need to acknowledge that we cannot accomplish this task on our own. We need God's help to pursue a relationship with him through Jesus, something that he knows all too well. Therefore he graciously provides for us, sending his Spirit of Truth, the Holy Spirit, to dwell in us and 'guide us into all truth' (John 16.13). Through the gift of his Holy Spirit, God gently leads us on into the realm of his truth, nudging us when we get complacent, encouraging us to keep going when the way seems dreary or rough, leading us into deeper levels of understanding, and reassuring us of his unfailing love and forgiveness when we know that we have failed.

Listening to the truth

Learning to listen to the truth about ourselves as God shines his light into our lives can be a rather daunting exercise. Many of us prefer to put a glossy cover on our painful past and plaster over all that is broken and fractured. Yet, as Nemeth says: 'we must be present to everything, the light as well as the dark. You can't choose to wake up just to the stuff you like.'[8]

Recognizing what needs to change within ourselves involves embracing both the comfortable and the uncomfortable aspects of our lives, knowing that we are loved without reserve by the one who made us, and that our identity is secure in our relationship with him. Only this knowledge makes it fully possible for us to bear the pain of our nakedness before him. We come to him who is The Truth, knowing that he loves us for who we are, not for what we do. As we allow his love to sink ever deeper into the arid soil of our hearts, he enables us to search for his reality, his truth as it pertains to all areas of our life, and recognize where we still need to grow. 'The more love we internalize, the more truth we can bear,'[9] and the more we know ourselves to be held within God's warm embrace, the more we are able to endure the probing searchlight of his truth as it sweeps across our lives.

'There is no fear in love', the apostle John reassures us in the first letter he writes from exile on the island of Patmos. 'Perfect love drives out fear, because fear has to do with punishment. The one who fears is not made perfect in love' (1John 4.18). Not only are we fully loved, we are fully known by God as well. Nothing we can say, do or think comes as any surprise to him. Therefore we can pray confidently with the psalmists: 'Send forth your light and your truth, let them guide me; let them bring me to your holy mountain, to the place where you dwell' (Ps. 43.3); and 'Search me, O God, and know my heart; test me and know my anxious thoughts. See if there is any offensive way in me and lead me in the way everlasting' (Ps. 139.23-4).

CHAPTER 5

USING QUESTIONS TO HELP
US REFLECT

'God makes everything happen at the right time. Yet none of us can ever fully understand all he has done, and he puts questions in our minds about the past and the future.' (Ecc. 3.11, Contemporary English Version)

Our thoughts are made up of an almost ceaseless patter of questions as we respond to life. Our answers to these internal questions help to determine the way in which we live. In this chapter we will explore the importance of our internal questions and of learning to stand still so that we can hear the voice of God. We will also consider how questions can help us to reflect on life and so draw us closer to God.

Central to our thinking

Questions form the backbone of our thinking. They are an intrinsic part of our humanness, an inherent feature of our thoughts. Each little decision we make, no matter how mundane, reflects the answer to a multitude of questions. Take, for example, the simple matter of eating breakfast, and notice the internal questions it may be based upon: 'What do I have left in the fridge? How long have I got? Should I opt for the usual combi-nation, or do I feel like something else? Where did I put the new box of cereal that I bought last week? Why is the milk already on the turn? How hungry am I anyway? Do I feel like making toast? What spread should I use? Is there any marmalade left or should I just have jam?' The internal dialogue goes on and on.

Most of the time we are totally ignorant of the internal

questions racing through our minds. On one hand this is very useful. We would quickly become overwhelmed if we had to consciously think through the multitude of questions behind every action that we take. However, if we are not careful, we can find ourselves running on automatic pilot for far too much of the time. We choose to blank out our internal questions and regard them merely as background noise, and we opt to rely on habitual ways of behaving rather than thinking things through afresh. It is then hardly surprising when we find ourselves feeling trapped, simply rehearsing the same old answers to the same old questions, and getting the same old behaviors as a result.

Cause and effect

There is a simple cause-effect equation at work. Questions provoke responses which produce behaviors. Our reactions to the world around are a direct result of the questions that go through our minds. It is a rather sobering thought. Our behavior, the unique way we respond to life as an individual, comes down to the internal questions that we ask.

We see this principle unfold with devastating effects in the opening chapters of Genesis, when the serpent uses a question to unsettle the harmonious relationship between Adam and Eve and God. 'Did God really say 'you must not eat from any tree in the garden?'' (Gen. 3.1) the serpent enquires of Eve, thus seeking to poison and undermine her positive view of God. By twisting God's own words into a venomous question, the serpent sows the seeds of doubt within Eve's mind, leading her to feel bewildered as she struggles to remember exactly what God had actually said (Gen. 3.2-3). From there it is a relatively short step for Eve's heart to become hardened towards God as she chooses to believe the serpent's poisoned words instead of trusting God. This then results in openly rebellious behavior as she, along with Adam, decides to eat the forbidden fruit (Gen. 3.10-13).

There is a stark contrast between the devious nature of the

serpent's question and the guileless questions that God subse-
quently employs as Adam and Eve try to hide their guilt from
him. He calls out like a slighted lover: 'Where are you? ...Who
told you that you were naked? Have you eaten from the tree from
which I commanded you not to eat? ...What is this that you have
done? (Gen. 3.9,11,13). God's questions slice through their
various excuses and pretences to reveal the real problem: sin.
Unlike the serpent's question which leads firstly to inner
confusion and then to feelings of guilt and shame, God's
questions overflow from his heart of love and help Adam and Eve
to think clearly once again. Thus God enables Adam and Eve to
come out of hiding, graciously making clothes to cover them,
using animal skins (Gen. 3.21).

Each of us will encounter similar circumstances which either
seek to poison our minds towards God or to build up our
relationship with him. We may not deal directly with a talking
serpent but the principle is still the same: the questions we
entertain within our minds will determine how we respond to
God, and this in turn will have a profound effect upon the way
that we behave.

It is something that Jesus himself is swift to recognize. When
his disciples' boat is caught unexpectedly in a storm, he deals
directly with their question of despair ('don't you care if we
drown?') so that their faith in him can be restored (Mark 4.40).
And when the Pharisees and elders try to catch Jesus out with
tricky questions about religious laws, Jesus responds to them
with further questions of his own to challenge their inner
dialogues and plant alternative questions in their minds (Matt.
15.2-9, Mark 12.23-24, Mark 10.1-3, Luke 12.13-17).

Standing still

With God's help we need to learn to slow down enough to begin
to unearth our internal questions, questions that are heavily
influenced by the varying emotions that we feel. We must not let

our emotions discourage us when they become too turbulent, for God constantly assures us that we have nothing to fear: he already knows us intimately and completely, and yet he loves us still. Moreover, he understands all the intricacies of our minds in a way that we never will. Nothing that we will ever think, say or do can come as any surprise to him. Knowing the truth of who we are in him gives us the courage to look ever deeper within, to hear the questions that arise spontaneously and to begin to discover why we react and behave in the way that we do.

God wants to help us see the errors in our thinking that drive us further away from him. In addition he wants our internal questions to draw us deeper into a relationship of trust and dependence on him. We must therefore learn to stand still long enough to listen to our internal dialogue and recognize the various questions that run helter-skelter through our minds.

Standing still, in a metaphorical sense, gives us the distance we require to observe our thoughts. It can be quite telling to pause for a moment and hear the questions as they rise up from within. Disjointed questions about the superficialities of life are mingled with much deeper, greater ponderings, while other questions demand swift answers as we deal with the pressing matters of the day.

This act of standing still is something that does not come easily to us in our modern world, a world in which doing, acquiring and achieving are prized more highly than simply being ourselves. Yet if we are to grow to become more like God and more fully the people that he has designed us to be, we must learn to cease our endless cycles of striving so that we can simply 'be'.

As we learn to stand still, the recurrent themes that drive our behavior, themes perhaps of keeping safe or searching for adventure, preserving the status quo or pushing boundaries, pursuing our own happiness or bowing to the desires of others all the time, can become exposed. Thus standing still creates a space in which we can begin to explore the murky depths of our lives, the receptacle into which God continually chooses to pour his incredible and undiluted love. In addition, it enables us to glimpse again the bigger picture of where we are going, so that we regain an eternal perspective on our current troubles and momentary worries. This is what the art of reflection is about: learning to be still enough to hear God's voice as he seeks to speak to us through our incessant inner questions.

Hearing God's voice

Recognizing God's voice within the circumstances of our lives is something that we all need to learn to do. Yet so often we attempt to drown it out, preferring instead to focus upon the questions that we deem more urgent, the ones centered around how we will get through our numerous tasks before bedtime and how we will make ends meet. However, if we learn to listen beyond those strident voices that scream for our attention, we will begin to discern the clear calm voice of God, quietly and persistently calling us to look beyond our daily conundrums and see his purposes at work within the details of our lives.

Perhaps we can learn something from Solomon here. The book of Ecclesiastes is full of his inner questions as he explores the meaninglessness of life. After some lengthy deliberations about the emptiness of all the activities people pursue, he finally concludes that fearing and obeying God is the only thing that matters, 'for this is the whole duty of man' (Eccl. 12.13). Thus his internal questions have fulfilled their role, in drawing him into a deeper awareness of his relationship with God.

A similar journey is recounted in the book of Job. Job is a man who faces a huge amount of suffering as God allows first his children and then his livelihood and health to be taken away. Despite the unhelpful questions of his wife and friends as they seek to short-circuit the process by offering him pat answers to account for his pain, Job replies with questions of his own as he explores where God is in the disasters he has suffered. As a result, even though God ultimately ends up plying Job with a barrage of unanswerable questions to remind Job that he, God, is sovereign, God declares that he is pleased with Job rather than with his friends because of his faithfulness (Job 42.7).

Journeying into reflection

For me the journey into reflection has been a long and arduous one, closely mirroring my journey into growth. Many years ago when I started my training to be a General Practitioner, being able to reflect on life seemed a distant and unobtainable goal. At that time I was embedded in a theoretical way of learning that relied upon what the 'experts' had found to be true. I based my beliefs on concrete evidence and facts, and my thinking was very black and white. I remember filling out self-analysis charts designed to highlight different learning styles, and realizing that I scored very poorly indeed on the reflective domain.

It was something that my relationship with Richard, my husband, had already highlighted. His aptitude for incisive questions had exposed my own inadequacies in this area from almost the first day we met. Yet although I had a vague feeling that I ought to aspire to be more reflective, I didn't feel ready to cope with the grayness of thinking that might ensue.

As part of my vocational training, I was required to keep a learning log. This meant that I had to note down significant positive and negative events as they occurred, reflect on them, and work out how they could inform my practice in the future. Writing this learning log was something that I found exceedingly difficult because it required me to look deep inside myself. I was terrified of what I might unearth, and so instead I concentrated on identifying clinical areas in which I felt I could improve. Nevertheless I knew that I was missing the point. The learning log was not designed primarily to induce guilt about my lack of scientific or theoretical knowledge; it was there to aid my personal growth.

The catalyst for change came in an unexpected form, in the sudden death of Richard and in the loss of my job. All too late I realized what I had lost. I no longer had someone to ply me with discerning questions when life got tough, or to help me reflect upon my life. Nor did I have the excuse of looking at my clinical practice rather than paying attention to the more personal aspects of my growth.

As I surveyed the ruins of my life, I knew that I would have to change. A radical overhaul was long overdue. If I were to grow through my experiences in a positive way, I knew that I would need to integrate the reflective skills my late husband had modeled so beautifully for me, and learn to utilize the reflective practices I had learned at work, even if it made me feel very uncomfortable inside. The unhelpful habitual inner questions that pulled me down and fed my deep-seated sense of inadequacy needed to be replaced. Instead I had to learn to harness my own natural curiosity to find questions that would bring me into a future filled with hope. I knew it would be a long process, yet I dared not put it off, for God was beckoning me. The first step was learning to slow down.

Learning to listen

This was something that I had been avoiding for a long time. For years I had been perfecting the art of keeping constantly busy in order to avoid dealing with the inner emptiness I felt. It was a behavior that had helped me enormously in the early stages of my grief, allowing me to avoid my inner turmoil until I felt more able to handle it. But as time went on I knew that I could not continue to postpone the inevitable. I needed to listen to my fractured thoughts and deal with them in a healthy way if I were to emerge from my grieving intact. This meant that I needed to pay attention to the little questions that were whizzing through my mind, and learn to use the little pockets of time I did have to myself to pause and reflect upon my life.

I felt incredibly vulnerable as I learned to make observations and assessments for myself without Richard by my side, and I often worried that my reflections were fundamentally flawed. Yet although my circumstances felt pretty hideous, it seemed that God was using my internal questioning to draw me to his side. He knew that if I were to be the person he had created me to be, then I would have to experience life for myself. I could only do this if I learned to ask questions of myself; questions just like those that my husband had asked me when we first met; questions that were incisive and thoughtful, gentle and revealing; questions designed to bring me into the future and not leave me in the past; questions that would draw out the uniqueness that was within me and allow it to unfold.

The questions themselves were familiar enough; I had sometimes used them in my medical work, and they were a fundamental aspect of the life coaching training I had decided to undertake. What was new was learning to use them on myself. It was as if God had gradually been allowing me to assimilate them into my life in a non-threatening way, getting me comfortable with them by first using them in conversations with others before he turned the spotlight on myself. How I winced and squirmed when the light was shining directly upon me. I didn't want to admit to the chaos that lurked within, nor did I feel up to the challenge of finding answers for myself. Yet steadily he shone his brightness into the dark recesses of my heart, willing me to look ever deeper within as he provided little pockets of time in which I could be on my own and slow down. They were like little oases of fresh cool water within a dry and barren land.

As I determined to direct my thoughts towards him, with his enabling, I began to recognize as if for the first time the truth that God loved me simply for who I was and not for what I could do for him. It was my being he was after, not my ceaseless striving for activity. Even though I was not yet fully the person he had created me to be, I could be confident that I was his and he loved me. This truth, that he knew me intimately and yet still loved me, gave me the courage I needed to go on.

Gradually it began to dawn on me that I had been slowly imprisoning myself. My own internal questions had locked me into a pattern of behavior that stemmed directly from my negative beliefs about myself and judgmental attitudes towards others. However I also recognized that God had placed the key for change within my grasp.Recognizing the truth of his love for me had primed the lock beautifully. Now it was time to ask God to help me to redirect and refine my internal questions so that the key could turn and I could break free from my habitually negative behaviors to grow more fully into the person he had created me to be.

Ontology

As I began to search for the questions that would free my mind, I came across the concept of ontology. 'Ontology is the study of being, in the sense of who we are spiritually. It's a compassionate and intimate look at who we are that includes the study of our true nature and what we're here to accomplish.'[1] Our ontological nature is 'a steady place inside of us that lets emotions and thoughts wash over it like waves but remains essentially unchanged… [It is] much bigger than our psychological make up. It doesn't change from moment to moment.'[2] This seemed to be the key. The questions I needed to ask myself were ones which exposed the ontological nature of life and dealt with the real business of what life was about. These questions were deep, exciting and open. They did not settle for yes/no answers; instead they probed to the heart of the matter giving rise to a sense of exploration and new possibilities. The jigsaw was slowly becoming complete. It seemed that my previous experiences hadn't been wasted and I could put my questioning skills to good use by turning the questions inwards. In this way my behavior would gradually come into line as I began to answer those questions for myself.

Asking deeper questions of myself required a lot of hard work. There was a constant pull within me to settle for the superficial rather than explore the deep. I found it very hard to switch from the easy questions that concerned what I was doing to the ones that had my being at their heart. My impatient nature meant that I often opted for full-blooded action instead of the relative inaction of choosing to reflect upon my life. But little by little God's warm love melted my heart and the overwhelming fearfulness of looking inside myself began to subside. Gradually I learned to stand still and let deeper questions rise from my heart, questions that concerned who I was being and who I was willing to become.

As I began to answer these questions, searching for the answers God had written on my heart, my understanding of myself increased, and I was able to focus more clearly upon God. In this way God enabled me to move forward into a new life which, although without Richard at my side, could be a life full of meaning and hope.

Questions that count

Learning to listen to God's voice and so reflect on life is something that can take a little practice and time. This process flows out of a deepening encounter with the truth of who we are in God. As our understanding of the truth deepens and we learn to listen to our thoughts, we can then begin to differentiate between the questions that will lead us in God's paths of life and those that will not.

Once again Jesus is our perfect example. In contrast to the serpent's closed question in Genesis 3 verse 1 that basically pushed Eve towards giving a yes or no answer, Jesus uses open questions that allow a wider exploration of the truth. He regularly responds to questions with further questions of his own to draw the listener into a greater awareness of themselves and God (Mark 11.28-30, Matt. 19.16-17, Luke 10.25-26, Matt. 17.24-25). And he often uses questions as starting points for parables or as teaching tools to invite a fuller degree of comprehension at the end (Luke 10.29-37, Luke 6.39-42, Mark 4.30-32).

Jesus' questions also enable people to articulate their need of him. For example, when two blind men defy the crowd and cry out: 'Lord, son of David, have mercy on us!' he replies: 'what do you want me to do for you?' (Matt. 20.32). Likewise, when a woman with internal hemorrhaging receives healing after touching his clothes, he asks: 'Who touched me?' (Mark 5.30). And when he sees a man in Bethesda who has been paralyzed for 38 years, he asks him: 'Do you want to get well?' (John 5.6).

In addition, Jesus poses questions to lead his disciples into a greater level of understanding. He asks them: 'Who do the crowds say I am?' before enquiring: 'who do you say I am?' (Luke 9.18-20). He quizzes them about his relationship to David and their knowledge of the scriptures (Matt. 22.42-46). And when a great crowd comes towards him he asks Philip: 'Where shall we buy bread for these people to eat?' in order to test him (John 6.5-6).

With God's help, we too can learn to reflect on life and ask questions of ourselves that really count. We can learn to employ open questions that allow us to learn more of ourselves and of God, and we can begin to formulate more profound questions that help us to focus on what is of eternal significance so that they can draw us closer towards God.

For some this process will flow most easily when time is taken to go on a retreat, to escape from the usual distractions and interruptions for a few hours or even a few days with the specific intention of listening to ourselves and more importantly to God. Yet getting away from everything for a while is not a prerequisite, for the art of reflection is open to us all. The questions in our mind flow ceaselessly enough wherever we may be. All we have to do is harness them with God's help, and improve their quality. Then, no matter how much or how little time we have available within our hectic schedules, we can use it profitably to direct our thoughts towards God. Standing still and reflecting on life can thus be woven into the pattern of each day just by using the minutes and seconds that we do have to make our internal questions count. By paying attention to our thoughts and focusing our questions both on our being as well as our doing, then God can help us to grow.

Reflection, like growth, is a continual process of learning; it will keep happening as long as questions can fill our minds. Therefore we must stay alert to our internal questions, constantly refining and modifying them as we see their effects within the behaviors of our lives. It is a process that flows directly out of a sense of personal responsibility (see Chapter 9). As we learn to accept that our ability to respond to life is under our control, we find ourselves being drawn into an ongoing process of re-assessment and re-alignment, a journey of reflection which asks us to observe the effects of our own internal questions on our lives, and to utilize their power and potency in order that we might grow.

The right questions

My experience has shown me that learning to reflect is more of an art than a science. It seems that there are no exact rules; each of us will come to it in our own unique and distinctive way. Over time the questions vary in their pertinence, and different circum-stances will require different questions. Yet despite the individu-ality we all display, there do appear to be some common strands. For example, a question beginning with the word 'Why?' tends to provoke a more defensive response than a question beginning with 'How?' or 'What?' In addition, questions that cannot simply be answered by a yes or a no will usually lead to a greater depth of discovery.

Despite all my searching, I have never found a definitive or exhaustive list of the perfect questions to ask, something that no longer surprises me: I suspect that there are as many 'right' questions as there are people. Below I have listed some of the questions that have been particularly meaningful to me; my hope is that they encourage you to think of further questions of your own. Here they are, in no particular order:

What is important here?
What can I be grateful for now?
What can I learn from this?
What is my next step?
How might this help me grow?
How might others support me in this?
How might this enable me to contribute to others?
How might this benefit the whole?

As with emotions, questions should never be seen as ends in themselves. They are merely tools to aid our exploration and reflection as we seek to grow.

Some people like to create their own personal list of questions for regular private use to help them stay in touch with what God wants to do in their life. For example, James Lawrence, in his excellent book 'Growing Leaders', quotes these four questions that he uses on a regular basis to aid his growth:

What is my next step in relation to God?
What is my next step in the development of my character?
What is my next step in my family life?
What is my next step in my work? [3]

Other people prefer to use reflective questions in a group setting or in discussion with one or two trusted friends. There is much value in sharing our reflections with other people as they can add greatly to the richness of our responses by reflecting back to us what we have said and how it has come across. These deeper questions can also be useful in building a strong sense of community and accountability between individuals. We will touch on this again in Chapter 6.

In terms of growth, however, the important message is that reflection, whether it is alone or with others, sporadic or a regular part of life, can draw us closer to God.

Journaling

One of the most helpful exercises I have found in aiding my own reflections is writing a journal. It is not a meticulous diary of events or even a considered response to the world at large. Rather, my journal is a place for me to let my thoughts out into the open so I can acknowledge the issues that I am wrestling with before God and ask for his understanding and perspective to fill my thoughts. As I write down my questions, often I find that an answer starts to form and work its way onto the page. Then, as I allow the process to unfold, I usually find that my sense of clarity and focus is regained.

I have adopted the practice of what Julia Cameron calls 'The Morning Pages,'[4] where I begin each day with writing down the numerous thoughts that are racing through my mind. As I do this, I find that my half-jointed ideas and unfinished thought processes are enabled to run to their own conclusions in a way that they would otherwise be unable to do. Everything gets included in those pages, no matter how silly or trivial they may seem, for my morning pages are not designed to be re-read by anyone else. Instead, they are opportunities for me to spend undiluted time with God, to listen to what he might be saying through the events of my life, and to attempt to understand the deep workings of my heart.

A personal journey

Learning to reflect on life is a very personal journey. There are many tools that can be used to aid reflection, and I am conscious that in this chapter I have touched on just one: the importance of deep (ontological) questions that address who we are being, and help to reveal what is really important in life. As we close this chapter, I would like to invite you to stand still for a while to listen to some of the internal questions that are running through your mind to see if there are any recurrent themes. It may then be helpful to experiment with some of the questions I shared with you earlier, so that you can observe the difference in your response. In this way you may become aware of further questions of your own that are begging to be answered, either by spending time on your own or by sharing the process of reflection with a friend. However you begin, I urge you to make a start, for God has placed so many profound answers deep within your heart, answers that resonate with his voice of wisdom as you seek to integrate the art of reflection into your life.

CHAPTER 6

THE ROLE OF RELATIONSHIPS

'As iron sharpens iron, so one person sharpens another.' (Prov. 27:17, Today's New International Version.)

God's love is the essence of life, and this love is expressed in tangible form through our relationships. God longs for everyone to be ignited by his love and compassion so that his glory can be revealed, and he has designed each one of us to fulfill a specific role within the functioning of the whole. This role is uniquely suited to us as an individual, and is worked out in the context of our relationships.

In this chapter we will consider how our relationships with one another can help us grow. We will look at the difference between individualism and individuality, and we will use the metaphors of scaffolding, signposts and anchors. In addition we will look at what it means to listen deeply to others and how we can improve our relationships with others.

Being church

The world is in desperate need of God's love, and as Christians we must seek to reveal that love through our relationships. Our relationships in their broadest sense therefore need to be a priority, far above accomplishing tasks and acquiring things.

The only human hands God has now are ours. He therefore asks us to act on his behalf, to show others the same love, acceptance and forgiveness that he has bestowed on us. We do this by being there for one another, as the body of Christ, supporting and affirming one another in love, learning from and with one another, and gently and graciously holding out the hand of friendship to all. This is what being church is about – working together to be the hands and feet and mouth and ears of God within the world.

When we are being this kind of loving, living, dynamic organism, a community that seeks the transformation of all God has created into the best it can be, we need not fear change. Being in relationship with others helps us to recognize that we are not alone in our imperfections: others have struggles and weaknesses too. Often it seems that we are much harder on ourselves than we would be on others in a similar circumstance. As we learn to be compassionate to others, we can learn to show ourselves compassion too. 'As we accept our personal limits and weaknesses, we discover that we need others and learn to appreciate others and to thank them.'[1]

The journey of our growth is, of necessity, an intensely personal one, and yet it is a journey that God does not expect or want us to undertake entirely on our own. Through our connections with other people he wants us to learn to call forth the most beautiful aspects of ourselves, so that we can together grow into the people that he designed us to become. By allowing others to minister to us in love, we can learn to accept the uncomfortable parts of ourselves and receive courage to move forward in new ways. We are called to mutually support and serve one another in a constant dance of inter-dependence, and accept that we are accountable to one another in some way. Our growth is a joint venture as we help each other to develop into the people God has called us to be. The proper framework for this is a recognition that we belong to God and are held securely by his love as we relate with others in his family.

Connectedness

We need each other. It is as simple and profound as that, for in the words of Benedict, 'we get to heaven together or not at all; there are no private compartments on the [Benedictine] journey to everlasting life.'[2] 'We all have to discover that there are others like us who have gifts and needs; no one of us is the center of the world. We are a small but important part in our universe. We all have a part to play. We need one another.'[3]

Everything in our world is related to everything else, and even the universe in which we live is itself intrinsically relational. In the past scientists struggled to explain the connectedness of all things. They could not prove the existence of something they could not see and barely understood, and so for hundreds of years it was left in the realm of mysticism because it was 'unproven therefore untrue'. Happily, this is no longer the case: the 'new physics' of quantum particles and fields of energy has been able to show that everything is indeed connected, just as the mystics knew all along.[4] This is something we will discuss further in later chapters.

Our interconnectedness means that we all have a role to play in each other's growth, whether our contribution seems incredibly little or extraordinarily large. Together we have the potential to expand and grow ourselves as individuals, to become more animated, more passionate, more generous and more able to reflect God's radiance as we relate and respond. In comparison, our lives are so diminished when we try to go it alone.

Self-awareness

Our connections with other people are vital for our growth. In purely selfish terms we need each other to be ourselves, to enable us to express our own unique individuality, for 'we do not discover who we are, we do not realize true humanness, in a solitary state; we discover it through mutual dependency, and in weakness, in learning through belonging.'[5] Our relationships enable us to 'break through the shell of egotism that engulfs us and prevents us from realizing our full humanity,'[6] and help us move from being purely introspective to being increasingly self-aware. As Abbot Christopher Jamison explains in his book 'Finding Happiness': 'introspection is only looking at me, whereas self-awareness involves considering how I interact with the world around me.'[7] He continues: 'This self-aware life does not accept that there is a private world of introspection and a public world of action. It insists that my interaction with the world includes my attitudes as well as my actions. This approach refuses to accept the modern belief that something is good as long as it does no harm to others. My own inner world is a place that can do harm or do good not only to myself but to other people as well. Simply being angry, for example, is bad for me and bad for those who have to deal with me; the vibrations of my anger affect others even if I never do anything bad. So self-awareness here means an awareness of my place in the world.'[8]

Thus self-awareness enables us to walk a middle ground between the two extremes, of either becoming so self-absorbed that we have little time for others, or becoming so outwardly focused that we lose touch with our inner world.

Horizontal and vertical relationships

We are intrinsically relational beings. Our ability to connect and relate to one another is an inherent part of our design, and once again it stems from our likeness to God. 'Let us make man in our image, in our likeness' we read in Genesis (1.26), thus revealing the perfect and loving relationship of the Trinity that lies at the very heart of the Godhead. The passage goes on: 'So God created man (i.e. humankind) in his own image, in the image of God he created him; male and female he created them.'(Gen. 1.27). The image of God is 'primarily corporate' and only together can we fully reflect God's image to the world.[9]

'It is not good for the man to be alone,' God asserts (Gen. 2.18), despite the unhindered relationship that Adam enjoys with God. For this reason a suitable helper is made (Gen. 2.20-23) to provide a reciprocal and complementary relationship which will enable them both to flourish and grow. Their horizontal relationship with each other is meant to flow out of their vertical relationship with God. It is given as a gift of grace, to allow the man and the woman to explore and appreciate the joys and frustrations of relationship in a more tangible form. In no sense is it intended to replace their primary relationship with God or to distract them from pursuing him as their central goal; rather it is given that they might together reflect God's image to the world as they help each other in their individual journeys of growth.

This upwards and sideways understanding of relationship is illustrated throughout the scriptures. Abraham, Isaac and Jacob are each called in turn by God to pursue their own relationship with him within the context of their familial relationships, and, as a result of their obedience, a great nation is birthed. As God's promise is fulfilled and the Israelites become ever more numerous, the strong sense of family connection remains, something that is heightened when they obey God's instructions to keep themselves separate from the surrounding pagan nations. Together they can then remind one another of their identity as the children of God, even when they are taken into captivity in a foreign land.

In a sense the biblical narrative is simply an account of their family history, a history which we are privileged to be a part of too as we acknowledge our identity as children of God. Our horizontal relationships within this extended family are intended to strengthen our relationship with God, and as we pursue our primary vertical relationship, it enlightens and spills over into our horizontal relationships so that together we can reveal more of God's image and glory to the world.

The importance of relationships

Relationships are, perhaps, the biggest gift that God offers us in this world, allowing us to experience the richness and fullness of God's love in a way that nothing else can. As we rub up against one another and become more aware of our own brokenness, God enables us to become more fully the unique individuals that he created us to be.

In the context of our relationships we can learn what it really means to love, to share, and to belong, as well as to encourage, to accept and to forgive. Our relationships call us to look beyond ourselves, to learn to give as well as to receive, and to allow each other to offer our own distinctive contributions as we grapple with what it means to be ourselves. In addition they provide us with a profound opportunity to bring the intangible qualities of God's goodness and grace into tangible form. Our relationships are therefore of vital importance as we seek to usher in God's kingdom on this earth.

Through our relationships we allow God to reveal once again his enormous love for the world. As we learn to live alongside one another in love, and see our own brokenness mirrored in the people that we meet, then God can use us as instruments of his peace, to bind up the wounds of those scarred by sin, to touch those who live in fear and pain with his healing balm, and to express his forgiveness to those who seek only to destroy and disturb.

In our relationships we can encounter the divine in a profound and tangible way, as we seek to minister to Christ in 'in all of his distressing disguises'[10] as Mother Theresa did, giving her life to serve the poor. By asking God to help us to look, like her, beyond the difficult and disturbing outward appearances to see the Christ within each person whom we meet, we too can be released from the pettiness of our awkward little lives to become a channel for God to work through.

Relationship

Our relationships are designed by God as the perfect forum for us to be ourselves, to offer ourselves willingly to one another and to God again and again, and to carry one another's burdens so that God's image in us can then be made complete. All of us have been endowed with the capacity to form relationships in our own unique way, and none of us can claim to be exempt. Our relationships with other people form the backdrop for the whole of life. Some might only last for a short season, and then we need to let them go; other relationships might come into our lives to fulfill a particular purpose, even if this is not obvious to us at the time; and still others may continue for a life time, challenging us and provoking our inner and outer reactions in the areas where we still need to grow.

The modern usage of the word 'relationships' can get in the way, for so often it is used to denote an exclusive one-on-one partnership with romantic overtones.[11] In reality, however, the word is far broader and richer than this. In essence it implies a connection, an association or an involvement between people, whether by blood or marriage, or in emotional or social terms. It derives from the word 'relation' (from the Latin *'relationem'* meaning 'a bringing back, restoring') and the verb 'to relate' (from the prefix *'re'*, meaning 'back, again', and the Latin word *'oblatus'* which has the sense of being 'carried or borne', as well as 'to offer or bring before').[12] Thus it not only highlights our affiliation with one another, it also promotes the idea that our connections with one another help to restore us as individuals and are a vital component of our growth.

Individualism and individuality

Relationships ask us to constantly give of ourselves in love. They invite us to bring our whole selves to the picture God is creating, and to take risks in being who we were created to be. In a deep sense, it seems that relationships are what life on earth is all about. The connections that we make with each other are far more important than anything we can do or acquire, achieve or possess, and together they help to define and refine us so that we can grow to become more like God. To use a construction metaphor, it is as if our relationships are the cement that holds the different building blocks of our life in place, helping to smooth out the roughened edges so they can fit together with greater ease.

There is no space for an individualistic approach where we look out for our own needs at the expense of others, whether we live primarily in a family, a community or on our own. Rather we must constantly seek to offer the particular gift of our own individuality within the relationships that we are privileged to make, in order that God might use us to have a positive impact upon the whole.

Even those who are called to live physically on their own can contribute by allowing their experience of journeying towards God to flow out to those around. The insights that they glean as they allow their solitude to draw them closer to God can be sources of much needed insight and wisdom.

The desert fathers and mothers who lived in the Middle East in the fourth and fifth centuries in conditions of extreme isolation are a shining example of this. In their physical remoteness they 'plumbed the depths of the soul and from those depths they invited people to look at spirituality in ways that are imaginative and challenging....They are remarkable guides, combining wit, insight and wisdom in a mixture that we moderns can only envy.'[13] The most renowned of these desert fathers was Father Anthony who spent 20 years in complete solitude during which 'the shell of his superficial securities was cracked and the abyss of iniquity was opened to him', something he survived only because of his unconditional surrender to God. 'When he emerged, people recognized in him the qualities of an authentic 'healthy' man, whole in body, mind and soul. They flocked to him for healing, comfort, and direction.'[14] His words of wisdom continue to inspire people still.

For most of us, however, the journey of our growth will take us through the marketplace of life, where our day-to-day relationships give us ample opportunity to experience both joys and frustrations. There, in the midst of our multiple interpersonal connections, we must be careful to remember that everything we do, say and think has an impact on the outside world and will affect others in some way.

Relationships as scaffolding

Relationships are not simply a coincidental or superfluous by-product of a world populated by people; they are part of God's explicit design, the very means through which he chooses to reveal himself through and in us, and they serve a multifunctional purpose.

Firstly, they can provide the scaffolding we need when our own lives are shaky. We all need assistance on occasions, for example when life feels hard and the way ahead seems uncertain or rough. At these times staying in relationship with others can provide the strength we need to keep going. We can then lean on each other in a posture of mutual support, forming a brace around the weaker parts, knowing that together we can be stronger. 'To be human is to accept who we are, this mixture of strength and weakness. To be human is to be bonded together, each with our weaknesses and strengths, because we need each other.'[15]

Going it alone is tough work. Just as long distance athletes must work together in groups to reach their goal, so too we must seek out travelling partners for the journey of our growth. In the same way that each athlete takes a turn at the front where the forces against them are greater, thereby enabling others to enjoy the relative ease of being in their slipstream for a while to regain strength, so we too will experience times in our lives when we are at the forefront, setting the pace and directing our gaze carefully so that our energies can be channeled into concerted forward movement. These are the points when we can feel the thrill of stepping out in new ways, pushing through the boundaries of our comfort zones, and taking risks as God seeks to lead us on. However we will also experience times when we need to tuck in behind someone else, to shelter for a while, recompose ourselves and refine our gaze so that in due time we will again be able to forge ahead. Allowing ourselves to form relationships that are supportive and loving, preferably within a wider community context, will go a long way in enabling us all to grow and flourish.

Relationships as anchors

Secondly, relationships can act as anchors to help us stay grounded as we travel through life. They enable us to stay in touch with reality and give us a greater sense of perspective. Together we can help each other to lift our eyes off the details that distract us individually, and glimpse something of the bigger picture of our lives. In this way our connections to others help us to stay connected to God. We experience his love and grace in action through the relationships we form, and he enables us to express these values ourselves as we commit ourselves to helping one another.

Having a secure network of relationships can also give us the confidence to try new things and reach out in new ways, knowing that others are supporting us in our endeavors to grow. Because we are securely anchored to other people, we can take risks that will bring forth the person we were created to be, even as we learn to be honest and vulnerable about our struggles and our fears.

In addition, being anchored in strong relationships with others can help us to overcome the debilitating feelings of despair when we fail or fall. Nurturing relationships in which our feelings can be validated and we feel understood help us to remember that we are not alone.

The anchor of our relationships can also provide the basis for an environment of accountability, where we are committed to moving forward and helping each other in our growth. Within the context of loving relationships, we can each give the other permission to challenge us by asking insightful questions to provoke further development (see Chapter 5). We can listen to each other in a deep way that goes beyond mere words, and seek the best for each other even if the cost to us is high. In essence, we can help each other to take hold of our heritage as dearly loved children of God.

Accountability is not designed to take away personal responsibility for personal actions; instead it acts as an external gauge of how well the internal process is going. It serves to further the personal journey by connecting it to the whole, and so ensure that we are together walking towards God.

Relationships as signposts

Thirdly, relationships can act as signposts to point to the truth. They reveal to us what is of paramount importance in life, and open our eyes to new insights. They provide a platform from which we can let go of the past, and invite us to explore the future in a new way, as well as encouraging us to keep going when we are unsure of our route.

The decision whether or not to follow these signposts is still within our power, and it is our responsibility to choose wisely. Making prudent choices in our lives includes not only deciding which relationships we will embrace and which we need to avoid, but also whether the advice we hear is right for us now. Surrounding ourselves with those who will selflessly encourage us to keep growing and developing will likely make the journey forward far smoother and probably more enjoyable too.

Observing the signposts in our relationships may not always be comfortable however. The path we are directed to may not look pleasant or inviting, and yet it may be the best one for the journey that is underway. Relationships where the truth can be spoken in the context of deep unconditional love are vital if we are to grow. This is tough love, the love that says that you are committed to the other person and to helping them to grow, even if that is not comfortable for either of you. It is the kind of love that God has for each of his children, where he is prepared to correct us and redirect us for our own good. Most importantly, it is the kind of love demonstrated by the cross, where Jesus took on himself the burden of our guilt and died so that we could become God's friends once again.

Listening deeply

Listening actively and intently is a gift that we can all learn to offer in love, both to ourselves and to others. Listening deeply to ourselves enables us to acknowledge our emotions and recognize the truth that God has embedded in us. In addition it helps us to recognize our inner questions and to reflect on life. Listening deeply to others can also serve a similar purpose as we allow them to articulate their emotions and their inner questions in a safe environment, perhaps for the first time, and realize the truth that they are unconditionally loved by God.

We can all choose to cultivate relationships where we can be honest about our feelings and emotions, our struggles and our fears. And we can all learn to listen to others unreservedly, putting our own desires aside for a time. Such deep listening is both expansive and powerful, and often leads to a greater level of understanding and peace. As the speaker articulates their thoughts without interruption, they are then enabled to delve deeper inside themselves to find the treasures God has buried there. Listening in this way is a powerful act of love. It says to the other that my agenda can wait just now in order to make space for yours. It affirms the person being listened to and allows them to expand internally so they can bring forth the best that is within them; and it permits the things that really matter that lie hidden under the external symptoms to rise up and have a voice. Loving relationships, in which we listen deeply to one another, thus enable us to acknowledge our emotions and inner questions, and to reflect on life so that we can grow towards God.

My experience

On a personal level I have benefited hugely from those who have listened deeply to me, and I am extremely grateful to God for providing such people for me. As I have tried to answer their probing questions, I have been able to hear for myself what is really going on inside and acknowledge how I really feel, and through their unbiased listening, I have been able to reflect on my circumstances and get more in touch with myself.

At times I have chosen to talk with trained professionals whose only agenda has been to follow mine. However I have also found it very helpful to talk to other skilled listeners, particularly those who would not be personally affected by the outcomes of any future courses of action, knowing that their observations could be more objective than mine. This role has often been fulfilled by my friends, a group of very special and unique individuals who have selflessly given of their energies and time, and allowed me to share with them my highs and lows, my struggles and my concerns. These friends have provided sturdy scaffolding for my life by surrounding me when I thought that I must fall; they have helped to securely anchor me within the storms of my life by showing me God's love in tangible form; and through their astute words and gracious actions, they have served as willing signposts to the journey of my growth.

Relationships and growth

Our relationships with other people are incredibly important. They provide plenty of raw materials for us to reflect upon, as well as reminding us of our interconnectedness and providing vital support, encouragement and direction. As we learn from and through our relationships, and listen to one another in love, we learn more about ourselves as individuals and so empower ourselves to grow.

Many of our struggles in life are connected with our relationships, and 'our reactions to other people teach us a great deal about ourselves.'[16] Other people can mirror our beliefs and attitudes back to us in a very potent way. In addition, other people's reactions remind us that we must choose how we respond to life (see Chapter 7), be willing to change (see Chapter 8), take responsibility for our own growth (see Chapter 9), and seek to align ourselves continually with God's ways (see Chapter 10).

We need to invest in relationships which will encourage us to take responsibility for our growth, support us as we step out in new ways, and take an active interest in our progress thereby helping us to stay on track. (In Chapter 11 we will return to this theme as we consider how we can help one another grow.) Surrounding ourselves with those who have chosen to overcome their difficulties rather than be succumbed by them can act as an immense source of encouragement when life is tough. Spending time with those who have grown through difficult experiences can empower us to move beyond our flimsy excuses and the fears which hold us back. We can all fulfill this role by learning to actively listen to one another in love, seeking to affirm one another as unique individuals and allowing ourselves to be used as channels of God's love.

CHAPTER 7

CHOOSING WISELY

'This day I call heaven and earth as witnesses against you that I have set before you life and death, blessings and curses. Now choose life, so that you and your children may live and that you may love the Lord your God, listen to his voice, and hold fast to him. For the Lord is your life.' (Deut. 30:19-20)

Before we move on, I'd like to take a moment to recap. We began this book by exploring the importance of growing and the fundamental role it plays in facilitating our journey towards God (Chapter 2). We then spent some time considering our emotions and how they enable us to respond to life in our own unique way (Chapter 3). Next we discussed the importance of encountering the truth with particular reference to encountering Jesus who is The Truth (Chapter 4), before we moved on to consider how to listen to our inner questions and reflect on life (Chapter 5). In the most recent chapter we looked at growth in the context of relationships (Chapter 6). Now it is time to examine the role of choice.

The decision to grow through life is one of the most vital choices we will ever make. As we choose to follow God's principles for right living, with Jesus as our perfect example, his love is able to flow in and through us to touch the broken world in which we live. This choice in itself is a gift from God to us. We can choose to leave it in its wrapping paper, admiring the patterns on the surface and leaving the seal untouched. Or we can opt to take the paper off, and discover what is underneath.

Growing up

When we were little children, our choices were necessarily quite limited and our caregivers took the greater load. While we poured our energies into working out which game to play or what snack to choose, they took on the more demanding task of deciding how to provide for our basic needs. It was their responsibility to help us navigate our way through the myriad possibilities of childhood, sometimes deliberately restricting our choices out of love, until we were ready to make all our decisions for ourselves.

As adulthood approached, this dynamic changed. We could no longer rely on our caregivers so heavily, and we had to learn to stand on our own two feet. It was up to us to build upon the foundations established during early childhood when we learned to make simple decisions for ourselves, and to understand, if we had not done so already, that each choice would have an influence on our future life.

Part of the work of growing up is learning to make increasingly complex decisions for ourselves whilst also learning to recognize that these decisions are heavily influenced by our emotions and our beliefs. Like our emotions, our beliefs are shaped throughout our childhood, developing steadily as we grow, and whilst at first we may simply choose to follow the principles adhered to by our primary caregivers, over time we must decide which beliefs we will adopt as our own. These choices are some of the most important decisions of our lives, for our beliefs about our self, the world and God will have a profound effect upon the way we live.

The best choice

To use another metaphor, growing through life is rather like building a house. Good foundations are laid when we choose to put our trust in Christ and declare publicly that he is Lord. It is then up to us to continue to build upon these foundations and to decide the kind of a house we want to create. We are faced with an ongoing choice: will we choose to engage with growing as a process, taking our time to select only good building materials and to lay them carefully on the firm foundations of our faith in Christ? Or will we opt for the less demanding route of throwing up the walls hastily, using anything that comes to hand? If we are wise we will submit our ideas for construction to a master builder and allow him to make the final plans. After all, God alone knows exactly what kind of dwelling he designed for us to be, and he alone sees clearly the bigger picture of our lives.

However, our decision to involve God in the building project does not stop at this point. Having carefully chosen our builder, safe in the knowledge that he is able to construct the best house, it would be senseless to go ahead without asking him to supervise. Only God knows the best position and precise order for each building block to enable us to grow tall and strong, and only he fully understands how to keep the walls straight and make the right gaps for the windows and doors. We need to work in partnership with God, choosing to trust in his life-giving instructions rather than the deadening safety and security of our own. Sometimes God will require us to make choices for ourselves within this partnership, and yet at other times we must allow him to intervene.

Growing through life is meant to be an adventure in which we continually determine to surrender our life to God. It is not simply a one-off resolution; rather it is an active choice that we must make and re-make every single day. We need to ask God to help us recognize that he is the best choice that we can ever make and that any growth we do realize is a product of his grace. In addition, we must continually submit the whole project of construction to his perfect care, giving him our undiluted 'yes' in all the different decisions of our life (we will return to this subject in Chapter 10).

Choices and consequences

Each choice has its own consequences, and we must be prepared to live with the repercussions of the choices that we make. This can be seen particularly clearly in the context of our health. The decisions we make about what to eat and drink, and how much we exercise, will have both short- and long-term implications. We need to have a sensible diet and drink plenty of water if our body is to function at its optimum, and we must exercise regularly and avoid addictive substances in order to stay in good health.

This same principle holds within the spiritual realm. In a very real way our choices determine who we will become.[1] How we choose to invest our time and energies now will have an impact on our present and our future growth. If we decide to ignore God's good instructions about how to live, then we cannot expect to enjoy the fullness and abundance that he promises to give.

Moreover our physical and spiritual health have a direct influence on one another for, as we have already seen, these two natures are intimately intertwined. God cares about how we look after the physical body he has given us just as much as he cares about how we pursue our spiritual health, and he wants us to be good stewards of both aspects of our humanity so that they may work together to draw us to his side.

In essence each decision that we make boils down to this: either we can choose to take the shorter, easier route of pursuing pleasure without regard for the penalties attached, or we can opt for the harder, more lengthy journey of growing towards God so that we might become clearer channels of his love and grace.

A countercultural act

Choosing to grow through life is a countercultural act. We resolve to submit our will to God's in order that we might become more like him and be transformed from the inside out (2 Cor. 3.18, Rom. 12.2). This journey begins when we first give God our 'yes', and it continues to take shape as this 'yes' is reiterated in every circumstance of our life. We accept the invitation he holds out to learn from life, even as we recognize that we need his help to live. Our decision to surrender to God is directly opposed to our inherent tendency to look after our own self-interests first. It also flies in the face of much contemporary thinking which attempts to persuade us that it is our right to do exactly as we please. This way of thinking often glosses over the dire consequences of self-centered behavior and conveniently fails to admit that God's declared ways of doing things, as exampled so perfectly by Jesus, are always best and always right. The recognition that God's ways alone will truly bring us life is one we must come to for ourselves, for although others can play a vital role in facilitating a wholesome view of God, it is up to us to decide what we will believe.

We need to choose to believe that Jesus is the author and the source of our faith, the One who supplies us even with the desire to become more like him. Knowing this enables us to trust that he will perfect the work he has begun in our lives, and bring it to its ultimate completion (1 Cor. 13.12, Heb. 12.2). On our own we can do nothing. Our growth is only possible in partnership with God. We must allow God to take his rightful place as Lord of our lives by continually choosing his ways over our own.

An awesome gift

When God first created man and woman in the Garden of Eden, he loved them so much that he imbued them with a very precious and special gift: the gift of free choice. This gift flowed out of his enormous love for them, for he knew that if he merely required Adam and Eve to love him in return, the result would be a very poor imitation of what was actually possible. In order for them to enter into a real and dynamic relationship with God, the desire to pursue it as a worthwhile goal would have to come from within them, and so there had to be free choice. Many of us know what happened next: that loving gift became toxic and was abused. Adam and Eve chose to listen to the lies of the serpent as he persuaded them that God was withholding something good, and so they ate the fruit of the tree of knowledge of good and evil that God had specifically requested them not to eat. The result was catastrophic: they were evicted from the comfort and security of the Garden of Eden, and forced to accept a life characterized by hardship, pain and toil. The relationship of love that had allowed them to walk side by side with their Creator in the Garden was broken by their disobedience, and their lives would from then on be a struggle as they sought to regain the intimacy they had lost (Genesis 3). Their urgent desire for autonomy from God had backfired spectacularly, and they were forced to live with the harsh consequences of their choice.

This removal from the Garden of Eden was, in reality, an act of love, for God knew that there was one other tree there that, although created to bring good, could now cause them harm: the Tree of Life. If they chose to eat its fruit, they would remain stuck forever in their sin, trapped in the physical bodies which now enslaved them, with no hope of ultimate reunion with him.

Today as God's children, we are still affected by their choice, for their deliberate defiance of their Creator allowed sin to enter the world. This fundamentally erroneous orientation towards God has permeated all aspects of life on earth, including each and every human heart. Consequently Eve, and in turn Adam, allowed their desire for autonomy to get out of hand and so forgot that God had only ever shown them love. In the same way we too can choose to challenge God's authority and ignore the fact that he is always working for our good, even when life does not unfold as we had hoped or planned.

The fact that God continues to imbue us with the same original and awesome gift of free choice that he gave to Adam and Eve is, in fact, further evidence of his immense love, a love that finds its ultimate expression in Jesus' sacrificial death upon the cross. Even though God knows that the gift of free choice can be wantonly misused and thrown back in his face, still he is prepared to proffer it in order that we might choose to love him for himself. Just as Adam and Eve had to decide for themselves what they would do with this awesome gift, so we too must decide. Will we use our free choice to follow our own desires, or will we choose to receive life from its source by deciding to follow God?

The source of life

The story of creation leaves us in no doubt that God alone is the only source of life. Nothing exists except that which arises by his command. All the vegetation and all the living creatures are brought into being because God gives them life, and as he makes his final masterpiece, the first human, carefully forming him out of the dust of the ground, God fills him with his own divine breath, thereby causing him to come alive (Gen. 2.7).

However God's involvement in life does not stop there. He doesn't simply walk away from the magnificent creation he has made. Rather he continues to sustain it day by day, laying down loving principles that will ensure the wellbeing of the whole. He instructs Adam and Eve to actively participate with his creative powers by bearing offspring to fill the earth, and he commands them to care for the animals and the plants that he has made. In addition, he sets in place a simple boundary in order that those he has created might enjoy their life to the full, without experiencing any fear or shame. 'You must not eat from the tree of the knowledge of good and evil,' God tells Adam, 'for when you eat of it you will surely die.' (Gen. 2.17). The catastrophic results when they do eat the forbidden fruit demonstrate conclusively how right God was. He designed life and brought it into being, and he alone was able to instruct Adam and Eve in the most fulfilling way to live. His prohibition is intended to restrict them in order that they might ultimately know a greater freedom, a freedom that allows them to pursue an unhindered and intimate relationship with their Creator, God. The alternative to this is death; a death that will creep insidiously into every aspect of their being, spreading brokenness, fear, pain and decay; a death that is brought on simply by choosing to turn away from the ultimate source of life, God.

This theme runs as an undercurrent through the whole of the Old Testament as God seeks to reveal his life-giving parameters to his chosen people, the Israelites. Lovingly he shares his rules for right living with them, in the hope that they might recognize that following his instructions will lead to abundance of life. Graciously he continues to provide for them, even when they reject him, because he longs for them to realize that his ways are the best. And passionately he exhorts them through their leaders to choose for him, for he is their life, even though he knows that they will repeatedly choose to go their own way instead (for example, Deut. 30.15-20, Josh. 24.15, Lev. 18.4-5, Lev. 25.18, Mal. 2.5). The book of Ezekiel paints a stark and dramatic vision of a valley of dry bones, portraying how dead things can become without God (Ez. 37.1-14). As Moses declared centuries before, God's rules for right living are 'not just idle words- they are your life' (Deut. 32.47). They are a 'fountain of life' to those who live by them (Ps. 36.9), and are capable of 'turning a man from the snares of death' (Prov. 14.27).

The greatest expression of life

Ultimately the greatest expression of life is found in the person of Jesus. He is the perfect example of a life lived in God's way. The opening verses of John's gospel express with beautiful clarity the wondrous truth that: 'In him was life, and that life was the light of men' (John 1.4). Only in Jesus, God's Word, will we discover what it really means to be alive. He shows us that the way to life is not found by satisfying our physical urges and desires but by feasting on God's words. 'Man does not live on bread alone but on every word that comes from the mouth of God', states Jesus, clearly quoting the Old Testament as the devil tempts him to use his divine powers to satisfy his hunger by turning stones into bread (Matt. 4.4, Deut. 8.3). After forty days and nights without food in the barren wilderness, Jesus knows that God alone can sustain him.

'Man's life does not consist in the abundance of his possessions,' Jesus tells his disciples whilst recounting a story about a rich fool who suddenly dies. Rather it is found in the wealth of their relationship with God (Luke 12.15-21). Nor should anyone waste their time worrying about what they will eat and wear, 'for the pagan world runs after all such things, and your Father in heaven knows that you need them.' Instead he urges his followers to seek God's kingdom and allow their heavenly Father to provide (Luke 12.22-34, Matt. 6.25-34).

Jesus' words to a Samaritan woman at a well are particularly striking. When she expresses astonishment that he, a Jewish man, should ask her to draw water for him, he says: 'Everyone who drinks this water will get thirsty again and again. Anyone who drinks the water I give will never thirst- not ever. The water I give will be an artesian spring within, gushing fountains of endless life' (John 4.13-14, The Message).

It is a theme Jesus picks up in the temple in Jerusalem when he addresses those who are there to celebrate on the greatest day of the Feast of Tabernacles. 'If anyone is thirsty, let him come to me and drink. Whoever believes in me, as the Scripture has said, streams of living water will flow from within him' (John 7.38). Later, as he speaks privately to his disciples to clarify the path that they should take, he announces: 'I am the Way, the Truth and the Life. No one comes to the Father except through me' (John 14.6). Jesus is the fulfillment of God's promises of life, and he is the only one who can lead us clearly in God's perfect ways.

Following Jesus' way

If we are to grow, we must look to Jesus, for 'he is the exact likeness of the unseen God [the visible representation of the invisible]' (Col. 1.15, Amplified Bible). By living in total dependence upon his Father, and allowing his Father's love to be expressed through him, he shows us how we too should live. Jesus is the only one who has chosen to follow the Maker's instructions faultlessly, and we would do well to emulate him, both in the little decisions we make day by day as well as in the larger choices we face. It is only as we follow in his footsteps that we can begin to grasp something of the fullness and abundance of life that God intends (John 10.10).

This decision is not always an easy one to make. Jesus tells the crowds flocking to hear him that they must be prepared to let go of everything, including their close family ties and even their own life, if they are serious about choosing to follow him (Luke 14.26-27). 'Foxes have holes and birds of the air have nests, but the Son of Man has nowhere to lay his head,' Jesus tells a man who declares his willingness to follow (Luke 9.58), while another man who wants to say goodbye to his family first gets this reply: 'No one who puts his hand to the plough and looks back is fit for service in the kingdom of God' (Luke 9.62).

Jesus repeatedly urges his followers to carefully consider the cost, just as they would before embarking on a building project or setting out on a military operation (Luke 14.25-30). When a rich young man enquires about the way to inherit eternal life, Jesus tells him what he least wants to hear: 'Sell everything you have and give to the poor, and you will have treasure in heaven' (Luke 18.22). Sadly the man then walks away; for him the cost of following Jesus felt too high a price to pay (Matt. 19.16-24, Luke 18.18-25). Contrast his behavior to that of Zaccheus, a swindling taxman who was so overwhelmed by a personal encounter with Jesus that he was more than willing to give up his considerable wealth. He recognized that Jesus was worth following despite the large personal cost, an action that caused Jesus to exclaim: 'Today salvation has come to this house' (Luke 19.1-10).

A broader view

Deciding to live life in God's way will inevitably have an impact on those around, for, as Zaccheus found, change is to be anticipated when we choose to align ourselves with him. It should therefore come as no surprise when we meet resistance as we seek to grow. We may rub up against those who have a vested interest in us remaining unchanged, because our growth disturbs and challenges their own status quo. What is more, we may be perceived as a personal threat or an intimidating presence by those who do not want to heed their own invitation to grow.

Rather than seeing these trials as a justifiable excuse for giving up, we need to recognize them as a call to perseverance, knowing that this in and of itself will further enable our character to grow. As the Amplified Bible puts it: 'Moreover [let us also be full of joy now!] let us exult and triumph in our troubles and rejoice in our sufferings, knowing that pressure and affliction and hardship produce patient and unswerving endurance. And endurance (fortitude) develops maturity of character (approved faith and tried integrity). And character [of this sort] produces [the habit of] joyful and confident hope of eternal salvation' (Rom. 5.3-5, Amplified Bible). It is the long-term view that gives us the impetus we need to journey on.

Suffering now and glory later on: it is the pattern of the cross as modeled for us through Jesus' life, death and resurrection. Jesus never said life would be undemanding; in fact, he promised that there would be troubles ahead, not just for him but for us as well. In the middle of a long discourse to his disciples on what they could expect to happen, he speaks these words: 'I have told you these things, so that in me you may have [perfect] peace and confidence. In the world you have tribulation and trials and distress and frustration, but be of good cheer [take courage; be confident, certain, undaunted]! For I have overcome the world. [I have deprived it of power to harm you.]' (John 16.33, Amplified Bible).

We must remember that the battle has already been won. One day we will see God face to face. 'Therefore we do not lose heart. Though outwardly we are wasting away, yet inwardly we are being renewed day by day. For our light and momentary troubles are achieving for us an eternal glory that far outweighs them all. So we fix our eyes not on what is seen, but on what is unseen. For what is seen is temporary, but what is unseen is eternal' (2 Cor. 4.17-18).

Focusing on God

Paul's letter to the Hebrews takes up the same theme, urging us to follow the example of those who have gone before us, and calling us to 'strip off and throw aside every encumbrance (unnecessary weight) and that sin which so readily (deftly and cleverly) clings to and entangles us', so that we can 'run with patient endurance and steady and active persistence the appointed course of the race that is set before us.' And why should we do this? Paul goes on: 'Looking away [from all that will distract] to Jesus, who is the Leader and the Source of our faith [giving the first incentive for our belief] and is also its Finisher [bringing it to maturity and perfection]. He, for the joy [of obtaining the prize] that was set before him, endured the cross, despising and ignoring the shame, and is now seated at the right hand of the throne of God' (Heb. 12.1-2, Amplified Bible). We choose to seek the path of growth, no matter how great the discomfort attached, because we want to draw closer to him.

Deciding to follow God's ways of growth requires ongoing commitment as we learn what it means to be patient in affliction (Heb. 6.12, 12.1) and to meet life with love at all times (1 John 4.7, 1 Cor. 13.4-8). We cannot afford to rest on our Christian laurels at any time. We need to depend on him for everything, and spend time regularly re-focusing on him as the source of all life and growth, and as our perfect example in every situation that we meet.

Our identity in God

Our decision to grow flows out of our identity in God. When we know that we are truly loved as his beloved children, then we will be willing for him to parent us. That might mean disciplining us when we go astray, or rebuking us when we get our priorities wrong, or it might involve showing us clearly the paths that we should take, or encouraging us when we feel low (Heb. 12.5-12). Whatever God is saying to us, though, needs to be heard within the context of God's love. God is love (1 John 4.8), and all that he allows in our lives is to be viewed from this perspective. He is not an angry parent wielding a stick to punish us when we do not listen to him. Rather, he is a loving father who longs for our return, wanting to bless us with good gifts from his hands when we follow his ways (see Luke 15.11-27).

We are privileged indeed to have a God who can identify fully with us through all our ups and downs because he has experienced human life from the inside. As if that assurance were not great enough, he has also given the gift of his Holy Spirit to dwell in us and reassure us of his presence and empowering every single minute of every single day (Matt. 28.20b, Heb. 13.5, Jer. 29.11, Ps. 138.8, Phil. 1.6). We cannot see fully as God does (1 Cor. 13.12), nor can we expect to understand all his plans (1 Cor. 9.9), yet we can be certain that he is constantly working for our good (Rom. 8.28) and he will not abandon what his hands have made (Is. 49.15), no matter how unfair or tough life might feel for us at any particular time.

The path of gratitude

Choosing to grow takes us on the path of gratitude to God. Whilst our feelings may not agree at first, we can still choose to remember that everything flows from his hands. Then, as we begin to see the abundance with which we have already been blessed, we realize that we no longer need to grasp and try to fix things for ourselves.

As we journey on with God, he enables us to accept deeper revelations of his love, even recognizing those gifts which are disguised in ugly circumstances and have many thorns and barbs attached. He accompanies us through our darkest nights and restores our hope again even when our hearts are filled with pain and fear. And when we find ourselves wading through difficult emotions like depression or despair, or our life has spiraled downwards and seems out of control, we can remember he is there beside us, and can use anything and everything to draw us closer to him.

Part of the whole

Our choices have an impact on one another, and living God's way minute by minute and day by day really can make a huge difference to us all. We are all interconnected, and even the tiniest positive action can be magnified into something that benefits the whole (we will return to this concept in Chapter 9).

Over the last few years I have become challenged on a personal level by the mounting evidence regarding the holographic nature of the universe.[2] Most of us have at some time seen a holographic image, a three dimensional photograph made by using laser technology. By definition, each part of a hologram contains the entirety of the information that is encapsulated within the whole. This means that even the tiniest fragment of a holographic image contains a minute version of the complete picture. More excitingly, if just one part of a hologram is changed, then the whole picture is affected instantaneously and in precisely the same way. Small changes really can make a big difference overall.

Likewise, our personal decision to allow God to work in and

through us, our choice to grow through life, really matters to us all. As individuals we have a part to play in the bigger scheme of things; this is part of God's original and perfect design. We have been given the incredible gift of free choice as an expression of God's love and grace, and when we choose to follow his life-giving paths and grow through life, we can help to bring healing to the whole. In the words of a song I used to sing at school, our prayer therefore becomes: 'Let there be peace on earth, and let it begin with me.'

CHAPTER 8

WILLINGNESS AND INTENT

'When he saw Jesus, he fell with his face to the ground and begged him,'Lord, if you are willing, you can make me clean.' Jesus reached out his hand and touched the man. 'I am willing,' he said. 'Be clean!' And immediately the leprosy left him.' (Luke 5.12-13)

Our willingness and intent are potent multiplying factors in the equation of our growth. Through them the significance of our decision to follow Jesus is magnified many fold as God combines our finite resources with his infinite power. In this chapter we will consider the inherent energy of our willingness and how we can harness it to help us grow. We will also discuss the power of intent and the importance of aligning ourselves with God so that the glory goes to him.

A willing partnership

Our growth is a joint venture between ourselves and God. On our own we are helpless; God is the only one who can change lives. However he chooses to do this through a process of cooperation, by inviting us to work in partnership with him. The Holy Spirit serves as a seal of this partnership when we put our trust in Christ (1 John 4.13), and through him the raw materials of our lives are blended with the infinite power of God.

Our willingness is the expression of our readiness for God to be at work within and through us. It serves as the dynamic interface between the human and the divine, coupling the physical realm with the spiritual to create an open space in which change can actually occur. It is like a delicate suspension bridge over the great divide between God's territory and ours, a bridge that is designed to support two-way traffic, as God works through his Holy Spirit to draw us to his side and as we seek to allow God greater access to our lives.

To use a different analogy, our willingness is like a powerful muscle by which we are joined to God. It is the means by which his redeeming power is coupled with our desire to be changed, thereby creating the opportunity for incredible transformation in our lives. The inherent strength of this muscle of willingness primarily comes from God, but it is up to us to make sure that our end of the muscle is tethered carefully so God can use it as he intends. In anatomical terms, he is the origin of the muscle and we are the insertion, the destination of the muscular activity, the movable part, for we are the ones who will bear the direct effects as the muscle flexes and extends.

Like most muscles, the more we exercise our willingness, the stronger it becomes. We recruit more muscle fibers to work together to fulfill the common goal. By declaring our willingness to be transformed by God, we are confirming our commitment to allowing God's purposes to unfold. We are expressing our desire to take God at his word and trust in his goodness and love, in order that his power might be revealed. Furthermore, we are proclaiming his ability to transform even our most appalling messes and crippling weaknesses into something beautiful for him. Thus by offering God our willingness we are, quite literally, enabling him to be at work.

Anchored securely to God, the muscle of our willingness contains within itself the means to produce change. It empowers us to launch out from the familiarity and the certainty of the near shore and begin to swim through the waters of our growth, even though we cannot see the other side. And it gives us the determination we need to keep on swimming even if the water is rough, because we know that our goal is worth swimming for. Our willingness thus becomes a clear channel through which energy can flow, almost regardless of our external circumstances and how negative or positive we feel. This energy, which arises from deep within, keeps us moving forward and gives momentum to our growth, acting like a form of courage as we allow God to change us bit by bit. The initiative is his, we are dependent upon his grace, and yet we too must take an active role. It is up to us to harness the inherent energy of our willingness and translate the theory of our decision to follow Christ into practice so that he can make a real difference in our lives.

Willing to change

The concept of willingness is one that I first came across several years ago when I was floundering as a single parent, desperate to move forward into God's future for me and leave the past behind. At that time I felt overwhelmed by the enormity of the task before me as I grieved for my late husband and came to terms with the implications of my widowhood. I found myself reacting badly to the children in almost every situation, being irritable with them instead of patient, filling my time with tasks rather than being available to them, and finding life far too serious and exacting to let go and laugh. I was frustrated with my seeming inability to change, despite fervent praying, and felt trapped by the limited energy supply I seemed to have. Life with the children felt like a chore, something which left me feeling angry and immensely frustrated inside.

During this time my coach nervously suggested that I read Maria Nemeth's book, 'Mastering life's energies'. The title worried me enormously, coming as I did from a strongly evangelical and almost fundamentalist background, but I was encouraged to put my assumptions to one side and to give it a try. I am so glad I did. It was as if a light had been switched on in my mind. Suddenly I could see the truth: I needed to be willing to act. Acknowledging my brokenness and moaning about what was going wrong on a continuous basis were not enough to turn things around. My focus was still on the negative. I knew I needed to change, and it seemed as if God was providing me with the tools that he knew I required.

As I read Nemeth's book, I saw the power of phrase 'being willing' as if for the first time. Simply saying those words aloud seemed to restore my hope and imbue me with a new-found sense of courage. Declaring that I was willing to change made me feel as if new possibilities were within my reach and it was worthwhile looking at different avenues to explore. By encouraging me to think of the positives I was aiming at rather than the negatives I longed to leave behind, I was able to look forward rather than look back. Moreover, by being specific about where I wanted to direct my willingness, my focus was being taken off the effort required and onto the outcome.

Trying and willing

Somehow it seemed as if those three words 'I am willing' were filled with their own inherent energy, an energy that I could harness to help me change and grow. They felt so different to the phrase I had been using, about trying to change. As I began to reflect, I saw that Nemeth was right: the phrase 'I am trying' had been giving me a ready-made excuse for bailing out, for failing to achieve my goal; after all, I had tried, hadn't I? However it also highlighted something else, something that her book did not directly address. By saying I was trying to change, I was implying that I could make the change myself. Nothing was further from the truth. I needed to repent and believe that it was only God and his transforming power that would enable me to change.

The expression 'I am willing' reminded me of my dependency on him; it showed me that I needed to couple my desire for inner change with his readiness to act. It felt as if God had placed the tools I needed within my grasp; I simply needed to use them.

Prompted by God through Nemeth's book, I therefore began

to look at specific areas of my life, particularly my role as a mum. I needed to work out what was important to me: what kind of a mum did I particularly aspire to be? What specifically did I want to introduce into my parenting? I came up with four words that encapsulated the essence of what I longed to be: loving, available, patient and fun; and I placed these four adjectives into the context of my willingness: I was willing to become a loving, available, patient, and fun mum. It was a sentence I could remind myself of daily, asking God to use my willingness to change me bit by bit; a sentence I could cling on to, to remind me of the person I wanted to become, using it as a guide rope to steer me through the waters when they threatened to get rough.

It was not long before I began to see results. I no longer felt trapped in a hope-sapping downward spiral of negative thinking. Instead I felt encouraged that a new and increasingly positive journey of learning was underway. Even more amazingly, how I responded to the children when they needed me began to change. Gradually God was enabling me to enjoy and appreciate the gift of motherhood in a new way, despite the fact that my circumstances hadn't altered. It felt as if God had met me at my point of willingness and through it he had supplied the energy I required to help me change.

Over time the phrase 'I am willing' has gradually transformed my life. I have used it in many different areas, to direct my limited energies and resources into becoming more fully the person God created me to be, someone who desires to live with authenticity and integrity. I have also found it incredibly useful as a daily reminder in prayer, to remind me of my dependence on God as my source and creator, and declare my willingness to be surrendered to God in everything and act as a channel of his love.

Willingness and faith

God invites each of us to couple ourselves with him through the muscle of our willingness so that he can work in and through us to transform and redeem. Bringing glory to God should be our central aim. We need to emulate Jesus who was willing to put his Father's intentions into actions by acting in total obedience to him. We do this by harnessing the inherent energy of our willingness and offering ourselves willingly to God. In this way our decision to follow Christ is converted from being an intangible possibility to become an actual reality with a specific shape.

The bible is full of stories of those who grew closer to God because they were prepared to take him at his word and translate their faith in God into concrete actions. In Genesis 12 we meet Abraham, a man who is willing to journey to an unspecified destination and make his home in a foreign land in response to hearing the call of God. Later, in Genesis 22, we read of his readiness to offer his only son, Isaac, as a sacrifice to God because his faith has become so deep that he is willing to trust God to raise Isaac from the dead in order that the promise of many descendants might be fulfilled (Heb. 11.17-19). Another striking example is found in the story of Joseph (see Gen. 37- 45). He begins life as an arrogant and foolish braggart, the favored son of his father, Jacob, which causes so much resentment in his brothers that they sell him into slavery in Egypt. Yet rather than allowing his circumstances to draw him away from God, he chooses to use his time to serve God diligently. As a result, by the time he meets his brothers again, he is willing to forgive them because he can see that God has used his circumstances to bring about a greater good (Gen. 45.5-8).

Hebrews 11 recalls many others in the history of Israel who were likewise commended for their faith, people like Abel, Enoch, Noah and Moses. They all demonstrate their willingness to take action because of their trust in God, even when it caused inconvenience and discomfort to themselves. The New Testament has many examples too. In Acts we see Peter and John continuing to preach about Jesus despite being imprisoned and threatened by the Jewish religious leaders (Acts 4.19-20). And later Paul shows his willingness to follow God's instructions by returning to Jerusalem, despite clear warnings about the suffering it will entail (Acts 21.13).

The supreme example is, of course, found in Jesus. He was willing to do all that his Father asked of him, even to the point of dying in excruciating agony on a cross, so that his Father's salvation plans could be perfectly fulfilled. Jesus commends those who recognize his willingness to act on God's behalf, often setting them free instantly from their misery (Luke 7.9, 7.50, 8.48, 17.19). And he urges his disciples to put their trust in him and believe in his power so that they can see answers to their prayers (Matt. 21.22). He expects them to act on the basis of their faith when he sends them out with authority to perform miracles (Matt. 10.1), and he assures them that they will do even greater things than he has done if they are willing to put their trust in him, because his intention is always to bring glory to the Father (John 14.12-14).

Intention

The word 'intention' comes from a root word meaning 'to stretch.'[1] There is a pull involved. When we intend to do something, we extend or enlarge ourselves, either tangibly or intangibly. We draw out our boundaries and propel ourselves into the future, going beyond the safety of our comfort zones, thus creating a sense of spaciousness inside in which new things can begin to unfold.

This is something that we have all experienced to some extent within our lives, for even the act of getting out of bed in the morning happens as a result of an intention, in this case an intention to arise. Whether we are aware of it or not, our intent has already enabled us to achieve many goals, both big and small. Our intentions can and do 'produce an energy potent enough to change physical reality.'[2] When we target our thoughts in the direction of a particular desire, it will come about.[3] Maybe this is what Jesus is hinting at when he tells his disciples that with even a little faith they can move mountains (Matt. 17.20).

Faith and intent

Our intent is very powerful, something that stems again from our likeness to God. In addition, we are given access to God's infinite power when we put our trust in Jesus because the Holy Spirit comes and lives in us. This means that when we act in accordance with God's will, his divine resources can and do flow through us.

Yet it seems that most of us live life in a state of utter denial; we are afraid to acknowledge the potency of our intent and see how great we could become. We ignore the truth that self-help gurus and manuals are all too keen to utilize, that in a very real way we are limited only by the size and quality of our thoughts.

As Christians, however, we need to be very clear that the power of our intent is not something to be exploited for our own ends. Rather it is to be handled very carefully and used only to further God's purposes and plans. We must constantly submit our will to God and choose to set our minds upon 'things above, not on earthly things' (Col. 3.2) so that we use the power of our intent to do only what his Spirit desires (Rom. 8.5). As Paul writes in the letter to the Romans: 'Do not conform any longer to the pattern of this world, but be transformed by the renewing of your mind. Then you will be able to test and approve what God's will is – his good, pleasing and perfect will' (Rom. 12.2).

Our intent must be grounded within the bigger picture of our faith in God. Our faith in him enables us to be 'sure of what we hope for and certain of what we do not see' (Heb. 11.1) and to believe that all things are possible with him, even if our faith is only the size of a mustard seed (Matt. 17.20). Thus our faith stretches us as we align our intent with God. And as we translate our faith into concrete actions by harnessing our willingness, his perfect intentions can be fulfilled.

God and intent

God himself is the master of intent. He merely has to speak the word for something wonderful to happen, to conceive the thought for something beautiful to exist. This is demonstrated most powerfully in the story of Creation when God says: 'Let there be ...' and then it appears (Gen. 1-2). In a similar way he provides sustenance for the wandering Israelites in the wilderness, calling the sky to rain down bread for them in the form of manna and directing water to pour forth out of a rock (Ex. 16.4,8 and 17.5-6). God's intent also provides miraculous pregnancies for Sarah (Gen. 21.1-2) and Hannah (1 Sam. 1.5-20) in the Old Testament, Elizabeth (Luke 1.13-25) and Mary (Luke 1.31-37) in the New.

This same power flows through Jesus, The Word, for 'through him all things were made' (John 1.1, 3). Jesus intentionally turns water into wine and feeds the multitudes, as well as healing the sick, casting out demons and raising the dead by simply uttering the command (for example Matt. 8.2-3, 9.2-6, 15.22-28, Luke 4.38-41, 7.9-10, 14-16, 8.28-33, 9.16-17, 37-43, 13.10-13). In all this he seeks only to do the will of the One who sent him (John 6.38), so that his Father's intentions can be perfectly fulfilled. In this way Jesus demonstrates that his will is one with that of the Father, something that he desires for his disciples too.

When he is told that his mother and brothers are looking for him, he reminds his followers of the importance of this by replying: 'Whoever does the will of my Father in heaven is my brother and sister and mother' (Matt. 12.50). On another occasion, when his disciples urge him to eat after going to procure food, he tells them: 'My food is to do the will of him who sent me and to finish his work' (John 4.34). And when Mary, the sister of Lazarus, is berated by Judas for wasting money by anointing Jesus' feet with expensive perfume, he springs to her defense, saying: 'It was intended that she should save this perfume for the day of my burial. You will always have the poor among you, but you will not always have me' (John 12.7-8).

Aligning our will

Our will needs to be aligned with that of God, for his intentions are always good and loving. For each of us the journey of inner transformation and growth will be very different, and our intentions will be distinct. However the call for everyone is still the same: to offer what little willingness we do possess to God, so that he can work through our unique intentions to bring glory to his name.

Our intentions reveal what is important to us. They point to the specific goals or actions which we want to achieve. The overriding intentions of our lives (our 'life's intentions') express who we are as unique individuals, and help us to become more fully the people God created us to be. They express our ideals and priorities in life, and reveal who we long to be. Our 'life's intentions' are 'the purposes or aims that lie in our hearts and give us a sense of meaning.'[4] They bring with them a sense of openness, lightness and peace. Our heart usually relaxes as we consider them for they reveal what is right about us, and bring our true selves into God's light. In this way they empower us to change and move into the future with God.

Discovering our life's intentions can take a little time. We begin by opening ourselves to God and being willing to listen to him as he speaks to us through his word, his world, and our reflections. Our emotions play a part in this process as we recognize that he wants us simply to be ourselves as he holds us in the warmth of his embrace. As we learn to respond to God's overwhelming love for us, he can then reveal the sort of people he is calling us to be within the myriad roles and relationships that make up our lives. He can also help us to formulate our life's intentions into words. Some examples are given below:

to be a loving friend

to be a gentle leader
to be a patient teacher
to be a courageous speaker

By learning to recognize the unique intentions that God has written in our hearts, we align ourselves more fully with God's purposes and plans, and so find a deeper sense of meaning and purpose in our life. Furthermore, as we focus on fulfilling our life's intentions with God's help, the energy of our willingness is tamed so that the glory goes to God.

Our willingness and our intent are powerful tools when we place them in the hands of God. Through them our decision to follow Jesus is translated into concrete action as we seek to grow towards God, and we begin to form the answer to the central question of our growth: with God's help, who am I willing to become?

CHAPTER 9

TAKING RESPONSIBILITY

'God created human beings; he created them godlike, reflecting God's nature. He created them male and female. God blessed them: 'Prosper! Reproduce! Fill Earth! Take charge! Be responsible for fish in the sea and birds in the air, for every living thing that moves on the face of Earth.'' (Gen. 1.26-28, The Message)

Responsibility is part of God's original design for us. It stems from our relationship with God. We have been given the immense privilege of bearing God's image and acting as his agents in the world. This privilege carries with it a responsibility to live in accordance with God's will. It is up to us to accept this responsibility and allow God to have complete authority over us as we learn to live in dependence upon him. Furthermore it is our responsibility to express the new nature God has given us through Christ by walking in obedience to him.

In this chapter we will consider our God-given responsibilities and the interplay between responsibility and choice. We will begin by discussing our interrelatedness with each other and our relationship with God.

Our interconnectedness

Everything in the world is interrelated. We are all linked to the entirety of God's creation in a very profound way. We are mutually accountable for the choices that we make, for our actions and reactions, including our emotional ones, have a direct influence upon the world in which we live (see Chapter 7).

The opening two chapters of Genesis paint a beautiful picture of a world in which everything is designed purposefully by God and nothing is overlooked or left to chance. All that is brought into being is deemed necessary for the completion of the whole, and the precise order of events reveals the meticulous nature of God's plans. First comes light, paving the way for all life forms on the earth to be born. Next the waters are gathered up to make space for dry land, thus providing the space for vegetation to start to appear. This is shortly followed by the creation of the sun, moon and stars to give seasons in which plants can grow. Only then, when there is a reliable and sustainable source of food, does God create the animals and finally humankind to rule over it all. The dynamic interrelationship of the different aspects of creation is clear: each separate strand of life has a specific function to perform that is essential to the smooth running of the whole.

Holographic images, in which every piece contains information about the whole, are a beautiful illustration of the powerful connections that exist within our world. As we touched on in Chapter 7, there is mounting scientific evidence to suggest that the universe has been created upon holographic principles: changes in just one area can have a huge impact on all the other parts. It is a phenomenon that is sometimes called the 'butterfly effect', as the example often given is that of a butterfly flapping its wings in one country leading to a significant weather change in a distant area of the world.[1]

Our external interconnectedness is also mirrored internally, for within ourselves we find a miniature world. This is one of the most universal of religious insights, and can be traced back to ancient times. As Origen, one of the great pioneers of early Christian theology, puts it: 'You yourself are even another little world and have within you the sun and the moon and also the stars.'[2] It is a truth that many in the West have been slow to allow, fearing that by looking deeply within we will lose sight of God as other than ourselves. Yet there is deep peace and wisdom when we recognize that all things can be found within us and are integral to us as a whole.

Throughout history many have sought to understand this mystery, often withdrawing from society to live in less hospitable climes. Yet it seemed to them that instead of leaving the world behind, they simply took it with them as they sought to live in closer communion with God. 'Far from society, alone, they experienced within themselves all the feelings, passions, yearnings, nightmares and compulsions which made human society so precarious, so turbulent, so fractured. In the silence they heard many voices within themselves, as many as argued and struggled in the world.'[3] It was as if their physical separation from the things of the world heightened their sense of connection to the whole.

Rather than filling them with despair, the struggles and anxieties they experienced within themselves came to represent for them the greater battle that was going on as God sought to redeem the world for himself. They felt within their hearts the groaning of creation as it longed to be made whole again, and they experienced within themselves the brokenness and pain of the world, recognizing that even within them a redemptive act was taking place.

As they brought their fractured natures to God for him to heal, they also carried the brokenness of the world. And by allowing God to touch them with fresh revelations of his love, they were somehow bringing hope and restoration to the whole. In this way God's Spirit was seen to be at work, just as he was in Jesus when he himself withdrew into the wilderness, producing 'intimacy with God, identification with the fallen creatures of God, always both.'[4]

It is a twofold principle: taking responsibility for ourselves flows into taking responsibility for the world. As we grow, God's Spirit enables us both to deepen our own walk with God and to identify more fully with the world around. When we bring our own brokenness and poverty of heart to God to receive his forgiveness and his healing touch, we are in some small and mysterious way helping to bring God's healing to the whole. Our growth as individuals matters to all, and how we decide to live our lives makes a much greater difference than most of us dare or want to believe.

Choice and responsibility

Responsibility and choice are like two sides of the same coin. Each is vital in its own way, and each is dependent on the other if we are to grow, but whereas choice can seem attractive and implies a sense of freedom and autonomy, responsibility often has a more negative slant. It is something that many of us prefer to shy away from, at least some of the time, for it seems to conjure up images of carrying extra (and often unanticipated and unwanted) weight, of curtailing our options, and of apportioning liability and blame.

The dynamic interplay between these two is apparent from the start. Adam and Eve's abuse of the awesome gift of free choice was simultaneously linked with an alarming abdication of their God-given responsibility to be his image bearers in the world. Neither of them was prepared to take the blame for what had happened, and so together they collectively tried to shift the liability for their actions onto the serpent and onto God (Gen. 3.12-13). The eating of the forbidden fruit led to their separation from God as they were forced out of the Garden of Eden into a life characterized by hardship and pain, while their unwillingness to take responsibility for their own actions would bear fruit later in Cain's sin (Gen. 4.6-7). Their freedom to roam safe and protected within the boundaries of God's estate was curtailed by their mutual lack of responsibility and their choice to disobey God; as a result they would have to work harder to survive.

Like Adam and Eve, we have been entrusted with a tremendously important task by God, for we too are his image bearers in the world. Our responsibility to show the family likeness is a 'given', a non-negotiable fact, just like our emotional capacity, but how we choose to interpret this fact is up to us to decide. In the same way that Adam and Eve could accept or refuse God's instructions for their lives, so we too must make a choice. Will we take on the mantle God has designed us to fulfill, and accept responsibility for how we act and react to life, or will we choose another route?

How we feel about taking on this responsibility is, in a strange way, almost irrelevant, for although God wants us to be honest about our emotions, he does not allow us to use them as an excuse. No matter how weak or inadequate we may feel in the face of this responsibility, we can be certain that it is something that he has prepared and resourced us to fulfill.

God's design

Each of us has been designed by God to take responsibility, both for ourselves and for the world in which we live. This responsibility derives from our unique relationship with him, a relationship that is meant to be characterized by an attitude of reliance. There is a downwards delegation of responsibility from God to us, for we are his image bearers in the world, created to work on his behalf by living in dependence upon him. It is only when we allow God to be God in our lives, and choose to trust that he is the one who ultimately bears the load, that our sense of responsibility can be properly fulfilled.

From the very outset of their walk upon the earth, Adam and Eve were handed positions of immense responsibility over all the other creatures God had made. They were instructed by God to 'rule over the fish of the sea and the birds of the air, and over every living creature that moves along the ground' (Gen. 1.29). This responsibility was intended to flow out of their relationship with God as they chose to work on his behalf. It was a daunting task which required much of them as they learned to exercise their God-given abilities and use the various tools and resources he had placed at their disposal. However it was the task which they had been designed specifically to fulfill, and God knew that with his help it was eminently possible.

By giving them this responsibility, God imbued Adam and Eve with a sense of purpose in their lives and a way of connecting them to the whole of his creation, as well as providing an inbuilt invitation for them to live in an attitude of dependence upon him. The weight of sustaining the world would always remain squarely upon God's shoulders, for the magnitude and gravity of the responsibility could not be borne in any other way. God did not want to crush Adam and Eve with a disproportionately heavy load, nor was he attempting to create avenues for apportioning future liability or blame. Rather, as a loving Lord he longed for them to fulfill their true potential by growing more fully into the people he had made them to be, and to take their rightful places as the crowning glory of his handiwork whilst learning to live in an attitude of dependence on him.

Playing God

Our dependence on God is critical: only he is powerful enough and capable enough to rule. We were not designed to take up his mantle of overall responsibility, and to carry the weight of the world upon our shoulders alone. Nor were we created to be omniscient, omnipotent, and infinitely wise. Instead we were made to be reliant upon God, to look to him to give us guidance and instructions, to embrace our frailty, vulnerability and limitations, and to operate out of the knowledge that he is in control. To quote Cloud and Townsend: 'Life only works when we are being human. It does not work when we are playing God.'[5]

'Playing God' is a very dangerous route to pursue, because it very quickly erodes our relationship of dependence on him. It is something we must resist at all costs, for it leads us on a slippery path downwards, a path that is ultimately heading for outright rebellion against God. And yet assuming the role of God is something that we attempt with alarming regularity. We try to tell him that we know best, that our plans are superior, our knowledge is greater, and we think we could do a better job. This is, in fact, a form of arrogance, and of idolatry. To even contemplate that our understanding could be on a level with his, let alone greater, sets us on a course that is completely contrary to God's life-giving path of growth.

What is more, when we 'play God' by believing that our opinions are infallible, we often end up sitting in judgment on others who want to do things differently, thus eroding our relationships with them too. Jesus has strong words for those who follow this route: 'Do not judge, or you too will be judged. For in the same way as you judge others, you will be judged, and with the measure you use, it will be measured to you' (Matt. 7.1-2).

Our circle of control

God does not ask us to control things outside of ourselves – that is not our business, nor our responsibility. Either they are his responsibility (in which case we do not need to worry about them), or they belong to someone else (in which case we should stop interfering). Realistically we have enough to do in keeping our own lives, including our reactions, emotions and behaviors, in check. Byron Katie puts this succinctly: 'I can find only three kinds of business in the universe: mine, yours, and God's. ... Much of our stress comes from mentally living out of our own business.'[6]

Jesus expresses it like this: 'Why do you look at the speck of sawdust in your brother's eye and pay no attention to the plank in your own eye? How can you say to your brother, 'Let me take the speck out of your eye,' when all the time there is a plank in your own eye? You hypocrite, first take the plank out of your own eye, and then you will see clearly to remove the speck from your brother's eye' (Matt. 7.3-5).

By focusing on what is outside of ourselves we are very close to missing the point: our responsibility lies at home. It is the contents of our own hearts and lives on which we will be judged one day, and our focus should be on asking God to help us with the carnage and debris in there. We need to allow God to be God, other people to be themselves, and to concentrate on what is within our circle of control.

Looking at the heart

Our responsibility begins inside, with what goes on under the surface of our lives. We desperately need to be made new from the inside out. And so we must come to God, for him to heal us and renew us and make us more like him.

The bible clearly tells us that whilst people often judge by superficial appearances, God always looks deeper, at the heart. Perhaps the most well-known example of this is when God sends his prophet, Samuel, to anoint one of Jesse's sons as the next king of Israel. Samuel is taken in by the fine appearance of Jesse's older sons, and he thinks they look just the part. However God tells him to pass them over in favor of the youngest son, David, a shepherd boy, because God has seen their hearts (1 Sam. 16.7, Acts 13.22).

God is not impressed by phony outward appearances. 'Produce fruit in keeping with repentance,' John the Baptist calls out by the River Jordan, urging his listeners to be made clean from the inside out (Luke 3.8). Jesus drives the point home, denouncing those who neglect to show justice and mercy because their hearts are far from God, likening them to whitewashed tombs which look beautiful on the outside but inside are full of filthy bones (Matt. 23.27-28, Luke 11.39-44). Skillfully he slices through their well-worn justifications and pretences, using scriptures to expose their hypocrisy and to challenge them to see that it is their hearts and not their hands which are 'unclean' (Mark 7.20-23, Matt. 12.35).

Excuses and blame

We cannot go through life blaming others, our circumstances, our upbringing, or our environment for the way we behave. Part of taking responsibility for ourselves is learning to accept that our propensity to sin is our fault, not that of anyone else.

Making excuses and averting liability are things that seem to come easily and naturally to us all. Even as small children we know instinctively how to attempt to wriggle out of blame. The patterns simply become more intricate as we grow up. As young children it can be reasonable to hide behind our primary caregivers at times, and allow them to take responsibility for us and our actions. But as we get older, we need to accept that we are responsible for our own words, thoughts and actions, despite the difficulty of the emotions that might be attached. Blaming others may offer us a quick and easy path out, a way of solving the immediate problem which absolves us from responsibility and justifies our behavior, even if it is less than good. But by continually seeking to apportion fault outwards we reject God's life-giving paths of growth, and therefore drive a wedge between ourselves and God. In this way 'blame keeps sin breathing and thriving in our lives.'[7]

Our relationship with God rescues us from this pattern and enables us to live another way. He invites each one of us to accept his love, as demonstrated through Jesus' death on the cross, so that he might wash us clean. This relationship is based on God's unconditional love for us, no matter how broken or sinful we have been. Yet it is also a relationship of total accountability, for when we sin we are answerable not only to the governing authorities but also to him. God expects us to take responsibility for our actions and reactions, not in order to save ourselves or make ourselves good enough for him – that is his role and his alone to fulfill by the blood of Jesus shed for us upon the cross – but in order that we might become more fully the people that he created us to be and so reveal more of his glory in the world.

A loving God

Living in this fallen world, we can never be fully immune from bad things happening to us and those around. We cannot always avoid disaster in whatever shape it may arrive, or expect to sail through life unaffected by losses and pain. What we can determine, however, is how we will respond. That is our responsibility, and it cannot be delegated or shifted onto anyone else. It is up to us to grow through the circumstances life throws at us and choose to see them as challenges to help us mature.

On one level this feels an incredibly unfeeling thing to say. I cannot know the horrible things to which you have been subjected, you may protest, and you are right. Each of us receives our own share of trouble and suffering, and some seem to be dealt a particularly harsh hand. What I can do, though, is tell you a little of my story which has brought me to this place.

As I have already shared, I was suddenly widowed several years ago. My husband of almost nine years died unexpectedly one night in his sleep. I was left with two young children to raise on my own. My life felt as if it was crashing down around my ears. In addition, my father-in-law died within a year, I lost my job, and I had to find a new home. Life felt totally out of control, and it was easy for me to feel that I had been treated unfairly. My circumstances had changed literally overnight, and I was spiraling downward in a sea of depression and despair. I felt battered inside and out by the storms I had encountered, and I was fearful and angry. Everywhere I looked there was wreckage, and the temptation was to throw my hands up in horror and wallow in my pain. However, God had other plans.

As I waded through the debris of my once-comfortable life, I became aware that despite the outward appearances, I still had a choice. That choice revolved around how I would respond to the events that had occurred. I could choose to blame God for it all and end up rejecting him as a result, or I could choose a more wholesome way which would ultimately enable me to grow.

In his mercy, God gave me the grace to accept the challenge of the latter path. Through his enabling, I began to see that his love required more of me than simply sinking into a pit of despair. He was calling me forth to become more fully myself, to take my place as an adult, and to take responsibility for myself. It was no longer possible to hide behind my role of wife or mother or doctor. He wanted more of me than the masks I had chosen to wear. He showed me that my responsibility for myself was just as great as it had been when my husband had been alive. In fact, it was even more urgent nowadays. I had to take responsibility for myself in a new way, and could not rely on others to do this for me any more.

God was asking me to be accountable for my actions and reactions in a deeper way. He was calling me to be a mature adult rather than a helpless child. He had given me the gift of free choice long ago at my inception, and I now needed to open that gift and learn to use it well. I needed to take responsibility for the patterns of behavior that were pulling me down, and the negative beliefs that I had justified because of my untoward circumstances. I had to trust in God enough to believe that I was his, and to seek his truth in my life if I were to overcome my difficulties. In addition I had to accept that I was powerless on my own to change; all I could do was come to him to receive his forgiveness when I failed, ask him for his help and offer him my willingness to grow.

As I chose to put my trust in God, my outlook began to shift. Decision-making felt less onerous and my fearfulness about the future was replaced with hope. In addition I became more aware of God's sustaining love and grace, despite the fact that life was still tough.

Gradually I came to see that God loved me so much that he was even willing to permit pain. He chose to allow the awful tragedy of my husband's death to occur, simply because of his great love for me. This love was tough enough even to risk giving me the pain of grief that could turn me away from him. What an amazing love that was. The only proper response I could give was to humbly accept his Lordship of my life, and choose to trust in him. I had to be willing to offer him what little I had, rather than hide behind the excuse of my pain.

The tapestry of life

Our ability to respond to life is a gracious gift from God. He is the one who equips us for this task by lavishly bestowing on us the capabilities we require. However it also requires us to do something too: make the decision to yield to him, to dethrone self and place him at the center of our lives. In the words of Cloud and Townsend: 'to humble ourselves constantly and to take the role of God's bondservant is the path of all growth'.[8] We do this not only by declaring verbally that Jesus is Lord, but also by being prepared to act.

Our responses to situations are our responsibility. Our actions and reactions are ours to control. We cannot change the events that occur, nor can we expect others to change to accommodate us. However we can change how we respond. We can choose to hide behind the role of victim, to resent the pain, and to medicate ourselves with unhelpful substances and behaviors. Or we can choose to trust in God's goodness and love so that he can help us grow. Seamands expresses this much more eloquently using the metaphor of weaving. He says: 'Life is like a complicated tapestry, woven with a loom and shuttle. Heredity, environment, all the things experienced in childhood, from parents, teachers, playmates, all of life's handicaps – all of these things are on one side of the loom, and they pass the shuttle to you. But remember, you pass the shuttle back through the loom. And this action, together with your responses, weaves the design in the tapestry of your life.' The loom is held securely by God and he directs us as we seek to move the shuttle back and forth. But, as Seamands continues: 'You are responsible for your actions. You will never receive healing for your damaged emotions until you stop blaming everyone else and accept your responsibility.'[9]

Life seems to have a way of recreating losses and pains until we are finally able to receive the healing we so badly need. It is as if we require many attempts to integrate the lessons they pose into our lives in a coherent way. The patterns need replicating over and over again to get the design just right as God seeks to weave his cloth through all the various warps and wefts of our life. And yet it is our responsibility to place the shuttle in God's hands in order that he might do his work in us.

Accepting our difficulties as challenges to make the tapestry more beautiful for him is itself the work of God's grace. It is an understanding that is not acquired easily, and one that many struggle to conceive. However if we are serious about growing towards him, then we must learn to grapple with this truth. We must learn to see the details of our lives as part of a bigger picture that God is seeking to create. It is our responsibility to accept everything that God allows, whether it is to our liking or not, and to respond to it in a way that honors him.

Being intentional

God has designed us to play a crucial part within his created world, and this means taking positive action whenever and wherever we can, within the spheres of our influence. We must therefore seek to grow in our awareness and understanding of the truth so that we can recognize where we have strayed from God's paths, and then we must choose to fulfill our responsibility to be stewards of God's creation, by living in attitude of dependence upon him. In this way we play our part in the healing of the whole.

Our responsibility to the entirety of God's created order demands that we be intentional about our growth. In order to do this we must know the goal that we are aiming for, and be prepared to take action to move towards it.

The apostle Paul likens life to running a race in which the prize is a heavenly one (Phil. 3.12-14). He talks about the perseverance we will need to overcome the various hardships we will encounter on the way (Heb. 12.1), and he urges us to run with a sense of determination and purpose, being prepared even to beat our bodies into submission so we can reach the final tape (1 Cor. 9.24-27).

I have the dubious privilege of living near to a university famed for its sports facilities, and therefore being surrounded by aspiring athletes. It has been very interesting observing which of these local athletes are really serious about their sport. Late night revelries and wild parties give the game away for those who are not fully committed to the cause. On the other hand, the ones who rise early to exercise before the heat of the day and are out training in all weathers can expect better results.

As we saw in Chapter 8, the root of the word intention is the verb 'to stretch.'[10] If we are really serious about reaching our goal, we need to be prepared to stretch ourselves like athletes in its pursuit. We might not like the disciplines we need to get us there, the things we have to forgo or the hassle we receive on the way. However, as Christians the prize we aim for is nothing short of seeing Jesus face to face; surely that is a goal worth being intentional about! Until then we need to constantly endeavor to become more like him by taking responsibility for our growth, whilst all the time acknowledging that any growth we do achieve is the product of his amazing grace.

CHAPTER 10

GOD'S PLANS AND OURS

'Trust in the Lord with all your heart and lean not on your own understanding; in all your ways acknowledge him and he will make your paths straight.' (Prov. 3.4-5)

God longs for all of us to work in partnership with him, fully trusting in his unfailing love and goodness as his plans and purposes unfold. These plans may stretch us and challenge us as God invites us to move into new ways of being and step to the edge of our carefully erected comfort zones. Yet as we express our own unique individuality in the little active steps that he provides, and become more fully the people that he created us to be, he enables us to give the glory back to him. The process of our growth invites us to joyfully rediscover the magnificence of our uniqueness. By asking God to share the plans that he has crafted individually for us and then acting in obedience, he is able to transform us to become more like him.

In this chapter we will explore how we can become more fully ourselves by cooperating with God's plans for our lives. We will begin by discussing the importance of focusing on God and recognizing the inherent goodness of his plans. This will lead into a consideration of how we can align ourselves with God's plans by asking, listening and depending on him. Finally we will explore the subject of worship as the truest expression of what it means to be ourselves.

Aligning ourselves with God

God is able to do immeasurably more for us than we can ever ask or imagine (Eph. 3.20) and he has already provided us with everything that we will ever need. All he asks is that we offer ourselves willingly to him so that he can breathe his life into the dry and brittle bones of our intentions in a vibrant and energizing way. In order for this to happen we must first learn to lift our eyes off our current difficulties and instead train them on God. In this way we are enabled to peer through the fog of our fears, frustrations and anxieties, and look beyond the obstacles that lie directly in our path, to see the small positive steps that we can take towards the new horizon that God is bringing into sight. We can then begin to translate our individual heartfelt intentions into easily identifiable actions that we can realistically achieve.

The journey of our growth is one of constant realignment as we choose to travel towards God. It is a journey which requires us to regularly check our compass bearings to make sure our north is fixed on God, so that we can adjust and re-adjust our course when necessary, using the landmarks of his love and grace. Like Christian in Pilgrim's Progress[1], our vision must be full of God and reaching his eternal kingdom, for only then will we have sufficient courage to walk the narrow path of growth when it asks us to pass between the sleeping but chained lions.

Life is full of potential pitfalls and attractive snares, each one beckoning us to step aside and leave the journey of our growth. The Great Bog of Misery sucks us in and cakes us with its mud, as if to reinforce our feelings of unworthiness to journey towards the King. In addition the charming trinkets and worldly pleasures on offer at Vanity Fair attempt to divert us from the path by promising to satiate all our desires with material things. Like Christian, we need to be constantly on our guard so that we are not distracted by the Enemy or ambushed by our weariness or pride. Moreover, we must seek to keep our feet firmly on the King's Highway even when the way ahead seems difficult or rough, for only then can we make it safely through the Valley of the Shadow to reach the City of the King.

Building carefully

We cannot escape the fact that how we live in the present will have a direct impact upon our future. Our current choices have an influence on who we can become (see Chapter 7). God calls us to build our lives with care and integrity, for he knows that each tiny detail exerts its own influence upon the whole. Each stone must be meticulously shaped and individually crafted before it can be set in place, and layer must be carefully positioned upon layer, ensuring that everything is in exactly the right orientation so that the construction might continue to grow. More is at stake than we might realize as we approach each tiny detail. We must not use shoddy materials or be short-sighted in the way we work, for broken bricks are much more fragile, and misplaced stones may start to fall.

Yet even if there are seemingly no disastrous consequences, then we are still called to build carefully, for nothing is hidden from God's sight. He cares for us passionately and is intimately interested in how we behave, and he longs for us to live lives of integrity, where we seek to honor him in all we do. The promise of quick and easy results should alert us at once to the possibility that we are straying from God's way, for he is far more interested in building for eternity than in any short-lived gain.

The simple fact is that life on earth has been designed by God to be a training ground, a place of learning and exploration and growth, full of experiences and opportunities to enlarge our vision and awareness of him. He therefore asks us to build with perseverance and patience as we learn to take a longer view, to see life as a preparation for eternity, and our current circumstances as a necessary precursor for what is yet to come. Taking time to regularly re-check our alignment and ensure that we are acting to further God's greater purposes is fundamental if we are to develop into the people that he designed us to become. It is the vision of future magnificence that drives us on, reminding us of the need for constant vigilance and honesty in each little detail, in order that the glory of God might shine through.

God's cathedral

The way we conduct ourselves day by day is of the utmost importance, for it is out of our mundane everyday actions that the
building of our life is formed. This means that we must choose
and place our bricks wisely and judiciously, making sure that
every one is good, sound and in accordance with God's will.

It is as if God has commissioned each of us to partner with
him to construct a magnificent cathedral out of the individual
details of our life. This cathedral is intended to serve as a signpost
to direct other people back to him. God works with us to create
the rudimentary framework of our building and hoist it into
place by helping us to formulate our specific intentions and
harness the energy of our willingness to change. He then seeks to
show us how to make our building less draughty, using the
details of our life to fill in the gaps between the struts of the
framework, thus adding strength and beauty to the whole. Each
building block, each minute element, will play a vital role as it is
levered carefully into place. But in order that the details do not
start to dominate or distract from the coherent splendor of the
whole, we must ensure that we keep building within the
framework of our cathedral and remember the overall purpose of
our individual construction scheme.

God's plans

God is both our direction and our aim. Not only did he
commission each of us to build a magnificent cathedral for him,
he also drew up all the plans. These plans were uniquely created
for each one of us, to skillfully blend all the nuances of our
distinctive personality and previous experiences into one
integrated whole whilst also providing us with limitless opportunities to express our individuality creatively within the details of
our lives.

The awesomeness of God's creativity within these plans is absolutely mind-blowing. There are no second-hand plans in God's kingdom, plans that have been designed to fit another but have now been forcibly passed on. Every plan that God creates is tailor-made for the one who will wear it, and he delights to weave all the intricate and individual details of our lives together into a unique work of art in a manner that we could never do on our own. His ways are always perfect, loving, holy and just (2 Sam. 22.31, Ps. 25.10, Ps. 77.13, Deut. 32.4), and his plans for our lives are always good and fulfilling (Jer. 29.11, Rom. 8.28, Phil. 2.12-13), for he knows exactly what we need to help us flourish and grow. He can use even the most unlikely building materials to create something beautiful, even magnificent, for the glory of his name.

God is the Master Planner, and his ways are so much higher than our own self-centered ones (Is. 55.8-9). In his kingdom there are no mistakes; everything is as it is for a specific reason, even and perhaps especially those things we find it so hard to understand. We simply cannot know everything that God knows, or see things clearly from his vantage point, for we are finite creatures, at least whilst we remain upon this earth, and our vision will therefore be at least partially obscured. All we can do is bow down to his superior knowledge and understanding and allow him to take control.

Depending on God

Our relationship with God is meant to be characterized by an attitude of dependence upon him, for he alone knows the best way for us to live (see Chapters 7 and 9). In him the past, the present and the future are one continuous and unified whole, and there will never be a time when we are outside his care. His plans are not a sort of insurance policy, to be cashed in only when our own ideas fail. Rather they are an invitation for us to look to him expectantly, knowing that he can and will provide exactly what we need.

To trust our own judgment rather than his is actually an expression of our arrogance; to seek to erect a cathedral out of the little pieces of our life without asking for his guidance merely demonstrates our pride. It is not enough that we look to God only in the big decisions that we make, for he is interested in every little detail. He wants us to work with him in the mundane happenings of our lives, just as much as he wants us to honor him in the big, momentous decisions. Every single circumstance is simply a further opportunity to surrender willingly to him and to glimpse the glory of his grace, so that we can experience the joy of working in partnership with him as his plans and purposes unfold.

The scripture at the start of this chapter seems to sum it up: 'In all your ways acknowledge him and he will make your paths straight' (Prov. 3.5-6). We need to grant God authority over every minute detail of our lives so that he can lead us in the path that he intends. Sometimes this process will seem quite straight-forward when God's paths appear to fit our unique temperament, personal preferences and gifts perfectly, and he clearly reveals his plans. On other occasions, however, God will choose to walk with us in hidden ways and take us on paths that seem contrary to our personality, inviting us to simply trust him and cooperate, even though we cannot understand.

Asking God

God does not want us to feel the burden of making plans entirely by ourselves: it is too great a job. Rather he invites us to taste his unfailing goodness for ourselves (Ps. 34.8), and to surrender the reins by which we seek to control the minutiae of our lives so that we might appreciate ever more deeply that he alone is the One who really can provide (1 Tim. 6.17, Acts 14.17).

Jesus himself tells us to: 'Ask and it will be given to you; seek and you will find; knock and the door will be opened to you. For everyone who asks receives; he who seeks finds; and to him who knocks, the door will be opened.' He goes on: 'Which of you, if his son asks for bread, will give him a stone? Or if he asks for a fish, will give him a snake? If you, then, though you are evil, know how to give good gifts to your children, how much more will your Father in heaven give good gifts to those who ask him!' (Matt. 7.7-11). We need to follow the example of Jesus who constantly depended upon the Father to tell him what to say and do (John 5.19, 14.24, 30, 12.49-50, 6.38).

God has been directing his people for thousands of years, and he is more than willing to direct us, if only we will ask him to. He does this through a huge variety of ways. Sometimes he guides people by speaking to them directly (Gen. 12.1-4, 1 Sam. 3.2-14, Acts 9.4-6), by giving them dreams and visions (Gen. 20.6-7, Matt. 2.13, Acts 10.9-16) and by prompting them through his Holy Spirit (Deut. 34.9, John 14.26, Acts 13.4). At other times he uses angels (Gen. 16. 7-12, Josh. 5.13-6.5, Luke 1.11-17, Acts 27.23-24), other people (2 Sam. 12.7-12, 2 Kgs 4.1-7, Acts 2.14-41), circumstances (Gen. 50.20-21, Ex. 13.17-18, Acts 28.17-20), and even animals (Num. 22.21-31, 1 Sam. 5.12). The number of options at God's disposal is infinite, so although we may not have a pillar of fire or cloud to direct us clearly as the Israelites did (Ex. 13.21-22), or be able to talk to God face to face like Moses (Deut. 34.10), we can be certain that if we acknowledge God as Lord then he will be our guide (Ps. 23.3, 25.9, 73.24, 139.10, Is. 2.3, 58.11). He will lead us in his 'paths of righteousness for his name's sake' (Ps. 23.3) and grant us the gift of his Holy Spirit to lead us into his ways of truth and help us to obey him in all the little details of our lives (John 14.26, 16.13).

Listening to God

There is not meant to be a great mystique attached to the process of discerning God's direction. Rather it is supposed to be as natural as a young child trusting that his parents know how to find the way back home when they go out. All it requires is that we place ourselves in a right relationship with God. To borrow a sailing analogy from the great American preacher and writer Jonathan Edwards, we can trust God to blow us in the right direction if we make sure that our sails are ready to catch his wind by listening to his voice.[2]

There is no point asking God to guide us if we do not listen to what he says. 'The real task of being true to oneself is a slow and profound work; it is not a fixed way but involves search and change. And in the end, being true to oneself can only be achieved by listening to God.'[3] We need to keep our eyes on the particular masterpiece God is creating with and through and in us, to celebrate our uniqueness and his care, and to actively participate in the intricate process of our growth. We must therefore learn to attune our ears to the voice of the good shepherd so that we hear him when he says: 'This is the way; walk in it' (Is. 30.21), for only then will he be able to lead us into the pastures that he knows will help us grow.

Trusting God

Life is a journey, and a good journey usually requires some degree of planning. At the same time it also leaves room for the unexpected and has enough flexibility to adapt to new opportunities as they present themselves. Trusting in God is the environment within which this process can take place. Our trust in him enables us to cherish each moment within the framework of God's bigger picture for our lives so that we can make best use of the opportunities that spontaneously arise within the little details and take the actions that he wants us to take. By combining obedience to God with using each moment as a further opportunity to worship him, he thus enables us to erect a cathedral that will bring much glory back to him.

Our asking and our listening must impel us to take action as we exercise our trust in him by obediently following the directions he has given us and allowing him to supply all that we need. After all, he is Jehovah Jireh, the Lord who provides. The question is: will we take him at his word? Will we trust God's directions for our life, even in all the little details? And will we trust that God is working for our good, even when we do not understand his plans?

The truth is that God delights in us, no matter how confusing or uncomfortable this may feel. When he reveals a path, we can be certain that he will also give us the resources we need to follow it. As Hudson Taylor, one of the earliest missionaries to China, often said: 'God's work done in God's way will never lack God's supply.' However it is up to us to utilize the muscle of our willingness so that we can step out in faith, for this is how we show our love for him: by accepting his guidance and doing what he says.

The size of our faith is almost irrelevant, for what really matters is where it is placed. When we put our trust in the One for whom all things are possible (Luke 1.37, Matt. 19.26), and take action as he directs, then our faith will come to life (James 2.26) and we will begin to change. We are simply asked to offer God what little faith we do possess, and allow it to move us into action so that he can do the rest. Then, as we echo the words of the father of the demon-possessed boy, 'I do believe; help me overcome my unbelief!' (Mark 9.24), and reach out like the hemorrhaging woman to touch the edge of Jesus' garment (Luke 8.43-48), his power and his glory will be revealed.

A threefold process

Making a plan is a threefold process: aligning ourselves with God, allowing him to share his good plans with us, and trusting him to provide as we take the actions that he suggests. All three components are needed for our growth, and each of them flows from a deepening understanding of God's love and grace.

To use another metaphor, it is as if God is holding out an

artist's canvas on which he wants to paint a magnificent master-piece, but as yet only a rough sketch of the outline can be seen. Only God knows precisely how to blend the colors and use patterns creatively to fill in the gaps between the markings he has drawn so that the picture really comes to life. Learning to stand outside the frame and view our life from an ontological, or greater than physical, perspective can make it easier to comprehend how the little details can play their part. Looking at the canvas through the lens of God's great love may enable us to appreciate the picture in a new and sometimes startling way, just as three-dimensional glasses can reveal hidden images within a flat landscape.

Our task is firstly to allow God to take his rightful place as Master Artist so that he can direct us in all the little decisions that we make. Secondly it is to dip the paintbrush of our willingness into the palate of God's resources, and ask him to help us move it carefully over the canvas of our life to paint in the specific details of our intentions according to his perfect directions.

Little active steps

The path of growth is an act of intimate cooperation and utter dependence on God. On our own it is easy to get overwhelmed by the enormity of the changes that we want and need to make. The intentions that we discussed in Chapter 8, those of being, for example, a patient mother or a generous friend, can seem so lofty and unattainable that we may be tempted to give up. It is rather like expecting ourselves to swallow an entire dinner in one gigantic gulp. Instead we need to divide our food into bite-sized pieces that can be chewed and savored one by one, a process that both aids our digestion and increases our appreciation of the food.

In the same way, God does not expect us to bite off more than we can chew. He is more than willing to show us when and how to break down our impressive intentions into reasonable mouthfuls, not least so that we can be full of gratitude to him as we successfully manage each one. He helps us to make a game out of hurrying to school one day rather than nagging the children not to be late, and gives us the energy to listen to them offload at bedtime even though we feel worn out. Likewise, he prompts us to buy a little gift for a friend who is feeling low, or take someone out for a coffee as a treat.

The steps that God suggests to us are always realistic and manageable, no matter how difficult or terrifying they might seem, for he understands our personal limitations and our distinctive circumstances better than anyone, and he knows exactly what we can do. He never asks us to attain the unattainable, or undertake tasks in which we have no option but to fail. Rather he invites us to work with him to achieve what is achievable and fulfill our unique potential as he provides us with all the resources that we could ever need. With his help we can take the little active steps that he suggests, so that in time our goals or intentions can be realized.

Being ourselves

God's plans for each of us are unique and individual, and the steps that he asks us to take are those that have been carefully crafted to fit our capabilities. What is manageable for one person may be totally unmanageable for another, and when we do succeed, it is by God's grace alone. We must be careful not to swell with pride at our accomplishments, or fall the other way into gloomy despondency by comparing ourselves unfavorably to others. We need to be alert to the opportunities that God reveals to gently stretch us in the right direction so that our greater aims can be achieved. Then even when the steps towards our bigger goals seem very small indeed, we can feel a sense of accomplishment as we achieve each one, and so feel encouraged to proceed.

We are called simply to be ourselves, to be the best that we can be, within the limitations of our own distinctive human frame. God does not ask us to be anyone else. He designed you to be you, and me to be me. This is the true work of our lives, to allow each other to be authentically ourselves, in all the little details of our daily lives, and to use our uniqueness to reflect more of the glory of God.

As we do this, we need to keep in mind that God is ultimately in control. Nothing and no one can ever thwart his plans (Job 42.2). 'A man's life is not his own; it is not for man to direct his steps' (Jer. 10.23). Although we may plan a course in our heart, it is the Lord who determines each step we shall take (Prov. 16.9). Thus 'life becomes the search for God's agenda in your life. When you find it, then you have found your true self.'[4]

This has been a lesson I have come back to relearn over and over again as God has drawn me onward through the extraordinary territory of my grief. My anguished cries of indignation are all too familiar to God as I have berated him about the perceived injustices of my situation, and he has endured many expressions of immense frustration as my grief has overwhelmed me once again. Yet so many times he has chided me as I have compared myself unfavorably with others, or sought to apportion blame, showing me that it was my attitudes that needed to change. Repeatedly, when I have tried impatiently to race ahead, he has sought to slow me down, using the peculiarities of my particular situations to invite me to surrender all my inner longings to him so that he might reveal his better plan. He has used the sharpness of my pain to bring me face to face with my own fallenness, and he has allowed me to pass through stormy waters so that I might realize my need of him. Through it all it seems that he has been gently wooing me, inviting me to look ever deeper inside, to rediscover who I am beneath the painful wreckage, and to recognize his lordship of my life.

Cooperating with God

It is now possible for me to look back with gratitude for all the opportunities he has brought. I can see that the seemingly unnecessary delays I experienced whilst selling and buying a house allowed me to gradually peel myself away from the past emotionally in a way that I could otherwise not have done, while the relentless stripping back of roles and friendships along with increasing amounts of time alone caused me to throw myself on God and learn to depend upon him in a much deeper way. The difficult decision to leave my medical career behind was made much easier as new opportunities opened up with the passing of time, and my ongoing discomfort as I continued to worship in the church where my late husband had ministered allowed me to feel a new sense of freedom when I finally made the move to somewhere else.

In retrospect, it feels as if God has used my grief to clear out the rubble of my former way of life. As I have sifted through my painful memories, it seems as if God has been sifting too, removing broken stones and damaged joinery to create a space in which he can begin to build a new construction. The foundation stones that he provided were the solid truths of his grace and love, certain and immutable and able to withstand any force. My task has been simply one of cooperation as God has done the work, levering the skeleton of his framework into place within my life. The intentions that he has given me have enabled me to harness my willingness and activate his plans, and the decisions that he has empowered me to make about housing, church and work have created a rudimentary structure to build around. Slowly the gaps are being filled in over time as I seek to honor God in all the little details and follow his guidance, so that the cathedral of my life can signpost other people towards him.

Worshiping God

Perhaps the most profound learning for me has been that God

does not want me to be anyone other than myself. As Thomas Merton wrote: 'Many poets are not poets for the same reason that many religious men are not saints: they never succeed in being themselves. They never get around to being the particular poet or the particular monk that they are intended to be by God.'[5]

It seems that God is calling me simply to be myself because this is how I honor him the most. To put it another way, I have come to realize that worshiping God is the truest expression of my self. Everything I do, including all the little details, is a part of my worship to him. I can honor him in my everyday interactions just as much as I can honor him in the big decisions of my life. The words of the Westminster Confession are so helpful in reminding me of this truth again and again: 'Man's chief and highest end is to glorify God, and fully to enjoy him forever.'[6] This is the reason I exist, to glorify God and worship him in all the little details (Rom. 12.1, 1 Cor. 10.31, 2 Cor. 3.18, Eph. 1.11-12). It permeates absolutely everything. There is no higher calling on my life. I must daily seek to honor him in all I think and say and do, constantly pledging my allegiance to him by submitting willingly to his plans, and intentionally depending upon him to supply all my needs, so that I may play my part in ushering God's heavenly kingdom onto the earth.

It is a calling that I seek to work out with much fear and trembling, for I know that I cannot do it in my strength alone. I can only become the particular person that he created me to be by recognizing that I need his forgiveness, direction and help. Moreover, it is only by his empowering and enabling that my life can become a beautiful cathedral that will direct other people towards him. I cannot spend time worrying about other people's reactions; my focus must be purely on God as I seek to obey him in all the little details so that his plans and purposes can unfold.

The bigger picture

This is how I show that I love God, by doing only what he

commands. My journey towards God is just as important as my destination, and life is full of glorious opportunities to learn more of God's love and grace. I must live each day in the light of my eternal destiny and seek to bring God's kingdom here on earth whilst I have the chance. The way I build my life right now is incredibly important, for through it I have the opportunity to reveal more of God's glory on the earth. When I choose to hurry headlong through my life in a mad sprint to the finish, I force myself and others to miss out on so much. The experiences and situations that I face are meant to be honing me, refining me and making me more complete, and the circumstances of my life are designed specifically to prepare me for my eternal task: worshiping God face to face.

When placed in this context, it is much easier to conceive that the situations I find so difficult may be in fact the ones that provide me with the best opportunity for growth. It then becomes more possible to accept the circumstances that I find myself in, even when they don't feel very pleasant, rather than looking for a way out. I need to remember that what I perceive as less than ideal conditions may not be regarded as such by God, for he sees the bigger picture of my life and he alone knows what I still need to learn.

CHAPTER 11

HELPING ONE ANOTHER GROW

'Be imitators of God, therefore, as dearly loved children and live a life of love, just as Christ loved us and gave himself up for us as a fragrant offering and sacrifice to God.' (Eph. 5.1-2)

Our growth is meant to facilitate the growth of others as we journey together towards God. This can only happen if we ourselves are in a personal relationship with the God of love. As we allow God to transform us by drawing us closer to him, he then enables us to become channels of his love so that we can help other people to grow towards him.

In this final chapter we will consider how we can help others to grow towards God. We will first look at the importance of our own relationship with God, before moving on to discuss the need for an ever-increasing awareness of ourselves, others and God. This will lead us to revisit the main topics of this book including the subject of transitions.

Our own journey of growth

'The journey of the Christian life is a journey into the love of God.'[1] We grow as we allow his love to draw us deeper into him. As our understanding of his love for us deepens, God changes us from deep within, and enables us to help other people grow towards him.

Our own journey of growth is vital. We cannot hope to be effective in helping others to grow towards the God of love if we ourselves do not know him personally. We must allow ourselves to be drawn by God by attending closely to what God is saying to us through prayer, worship and bible study; and we must learn to recognize the plentiful signs of his love as he constantly seeks to reveal it everywhere. 'Our first and foremost task is to faithfully care for the inward fire so that when it is really needed it can offer warmth and light to lost travellers.'[2] Jesus tells us: 'I am the vine and you are the branches. If a man remains in me and I in him, he will bear much fruit; apart from me you can do nothing' (John 15.5). Our relationship with him is critical. We cannot hope to draw others to the One who is the source of life if we ourselves are not intimately connected to him.

We grow not just for our own benefit but also for the benefit of others. 'This is love: not that we loved God but that he loved us and sent his Son to be an atoning sacrifice for our sins. Dear friends, since God so loved us, we also ought to love one another' (1 John 4.11). 'We love because he first loved us' (1 John 4.19). As we learn to accept the purity of God's selfless love for us and respond to it by walking in obedience to him, God then enables us in turn to love others with his love and help them grow towards him.

God is love

God longs for everyone to know him personally as the God of love. 'God is love. Whoever lives in love lives in God, and God in him' (1 John 4.16b). Constantly he seeks to reveal his love through his actions everywhere. The initiative is always his. He is the one who continually reaches out to us when we are still far off and persistently draws us to his side so that we can know the magnitude of his great love.

The entire story of salvation, starting with Adam and Eve and ending with Jesus, bears witness to this fact. In love, God creates a partner for Adam in the shape of Eve, gives instructions to Noah to save him and his family from a flood, and chooses Abraham to father a new nation of people to be the particular recipients of his special care. In love, God fulfills this promise by giving Abraham a son in his old age, and continues to make himself known personally to Abraham's progeny. In love, God rescues his people from the hands of the Egyptians, gives them instructions so that they may live prosperously, and disciplines them when they choose to live a different way. In love, God answers their cries for deliverance by repeatedly raising up faithful prophets and kings to lead them. Finally, in love, he sends his only son, Jesus, to live with them and die for them to conclusively demonstrate the depth of his love by dealing once and for all with the problem of sin and making it possible for everyone to be in right relationship with him. His love then bursts forth in resurrection power and raises Jesus from the dead, so that all may have the opportunity to be with him and experience his future glory.

God continues to express his love actively to us today. He lovingly sustains his creation day by day; he provides us with all that we will ever need to follow him; he leads us and disciplines us so that we can become more like him; and he delights to shower us with good gifts as tokens of his love even when we are slow to recognize them as such. In love, he also invites us to reciprocate his love so that we might know the joy of being in relationship with him, and help others to discover his love too. Yet even when we choose not to respond to him with love, he continues to inundate us with demonstrations of his love for it is his nature always to do so.

Awareness

We live in a God-bathed world and the whole of creation is alive with the presence of God as he seeks to reveal himself as the God of love. Our growth is a journey into an ever-increasing awareness of God's presence and activity within us and within the world. We are called to be like little children in the way that we view life, to gaze in wonder at God's incredible creation, to delight in the uniqueness of each person, and to experience life as always new, spontaneous and fresh. We need each other's help to grow in awareness so that we can fully appreciate the wonderful world in which we live.

Each of us has a different set of lenses through which we view life. We are the product of our upbringing, and, either consciously or unconsciously, we have been programmed to look at others through the lenses of our prejudices and respond to situations according to how they can meet our needs. As a result, our thinking is riddled with misconceptions and our vision is terribly impaired, so much so that even our motivations for helping others can be incredibly mixed. Most of the time, however, we are completely oblivious to the distorting lenses and previous conditioning which cause us to react unthinkingly to life. 'The unaware life is a mechanical life. It's not human, it's programmed, conditioned.'[3]

Not only do we need one another's help to recognize our own distorting lenses and unhelpful conditioning, we also need one another to help us to become more aware of God. The two are inextricably intertwined. John Calvin argued: 'There is no deep knowing of God apart from a deep knowing of self and no deep knowing of self apart from a deep knowing of God.'[4] We grow both by becoming more aware of ourselves and our imperfections, as well as by becoming more aware of the perfect love and presence of God.

Growing in awareness is thus a communal process. 'We discover who we are face-to-face and side-by-side with others in work, love and learning'[5], in the context of our relationships, and as our self-awareness develops, we become more aware of God. We need each other to see clearly, to help us see things as they really are. Through our interactions with one another we can become more aware of our distorting lenses and unhelpful conditioning, at the same time as becoming more aware of 'the already present activity of God.'[6] As we come face to face with our own imperfections, we gain a deeper appreciation of our need of God. And as we spend time in worship, prayer and bible study, both individually and corporately, growing in our awareness of God, we are then more able to see others as God sees them, as worthy objects of his love.

Developing awareness

Developing awareness closely mirrors the journey of our growth. It requires us to acknowledge our difficult emotions; to encounter the truth within each situation that we meet; to allow our questions to draw us towards God; to seek to honor him within our relationships; to choose to follow Jesus as The Way, The Truth and The Life; to be willing to change and to be changed; to take responsibility for ourselves; and to cooperate with God's plans within the details of our lives. Each of the building blocks to growth offers us the opportunity to increase our understanding of ourselves and God, and to allow his Holy Spirit to be at work. As our awareness develops, we can then use what we have learnt to assist others in their growth.

We all need to cultivate supportive, trusting relationships in which we can help each other to remain alert to the presence and activity of the Holy Spirit. By listening to one another in an atmosphere of love, we can learn together to hear the voice of God. By helping each other to become aware of our emotions and our inner questions, we enable each other to recognize where our responses are a result of unhelpful conditioning; and by helping each other to encounter the truth of God's unconditional love and align ourselves with him, we empower each other to respond to life in a more positive way.

Developing awareness can be painful as our illusions are shattered and we come face to face with the truth of our own inner poverty and need. We must learn to provide a safe place for one another in which we can acknowledge our diverse emotions and explore our inner questions as we reflect on life and work out what to do. This listening can be done informally within our existing friendships as we share the details of our lives. It can also occur in a more formal setting, for example, by meeting with a pastor, coach, mentor or spiritual director. In all these contexts the essential person is the Holy Spirit, who is always present with us and ready to act as our guide. He leads us in God's ways of truth and helps us to recognize God's voice as he seeks to be active in our life.

We must learn to put our own agendas to one side from time to time so that we can actively listen to other people as well as hear God. 'As we listen to each other we are also listening to God, for what we are seeking is to hear and recognize the voice of God in the midst of our ordinary lives.'[7] By listening to one another, both verbally and non-verbally, we can pick up recurrent patterns and themes, and by reflecting these back to the other person, we can enable their awareness of themselves and God to increase. In addition, by staying attuned to the Holy Spirit and aligning ourselves with The Truth as found in Jesus, we may be able to make pertinent observations and give timely words of encouragement from God that will enable the other person to change.

Awareness and choice

Growing in awareness is an active process which requires us to make an ongoing choice. Just as each of us needs to make a conscious and continual decision to keep following God, so too we must choose to constantly open ourselves to his presence and offer him our willingness to be transformed in order that he might reveal himself to and through us as the God of love. As we do this on an individual level, we can then help others to grow towards God by becoming clearer channels of his love.

Our decision to follow Jesus is a life-giving act. By living according to God's instructions, we benefit others as well as ourselves. Even though our circle of influence may feel quite small, we need to remember that we are all inter-related and our choices have repercussions which affect the whole. As we learn to follow God's instructions and make life-giving choices that will help us grow, we become more able to help others walk in obedience to God and make life-giving choices also. Likewise, as we learn to translate these choices into actions by exercising the muscle of our willingness and allowing God to work through the power of our intent, we are in a position to help and encourage others as they seek to make positive changes too.

We have a responsibility not only to make sure that we ourselves are growing, but also to help other people journey towards God. We do this by helping each other to make life-giving choices which will bring blessing to the whole, as well as by supporting and encouraging one another as we exercise our willingness so that God's perfect plans and purposes can unfold.

Growing together through life

Growing is a journey which leads us back to God. It is a journey which we undertake together so that all may know the God of love. By helping one another to acknowledge our emotions and encounter the truth of our relationship to God, we are more able to make good endings with the past; and by supporting one another as we explore our own inner questions and seek to align ourselves with God, we enable each other to negotiate the uncertainty of the neutral zone. In this way we empower one another to move forward in our growth so that, in time, the fresh green shoots of new beginnings may be seen. As we help one another to grow through our transitions, we act as channels of God's love; and as we allow God to work in and through us, he enables us to help each other become more like him and more fully the people that he designed us to become.

NOTES

CHAPTER 1
1   The song of the king. Max Lucado.
2   Transitions: making sense of life's changes. William Bridges.
3   p59. Managing transitions. William Bridges.

CHAPTER 2
1   Treasures of the snow. Patricia St.John

CHAPTER 3
1   p12. Managing your emotions. Erwin Lutzer.
2   p132. Molecules of emotion. Candace Pert.
3   Interestingly, what the bible has been telling us for years about the integral nature of our emotions is now being corroborated by modern science. Instead of our emotions being generated purely from one discrete place deep within the brain, or indeed a specific point anywhere else in the body, there appears to be a vast collection of information carrying chemicals, called peptides, which are widely distributed throughout the whole of the human body. These so-called 'molecules of emotion' act as a communication network that integrates the whole body-mind response, whilst also filtering out unnecessary messages, thus enabling us to perceive the reality in which we live. For more detailed information see 'Molecules of Emotion' by Candace Pert.
4   I am indebted to Noel Moules and his excellent exposition on biblical models of personhood, as given on the 'Workshop' course I attended many years ago.
5   For a fuller discussion of this see Tim Chester's 'The ordinary hero', p119-129.
6   p192-3. Molecules of emotion. Candace Pert.

7   p13. Managing your emotions. Erwin Lutzer.

8   p10. Ibid.

9   p8. Ibid.

CHAPTER 4

1   p37. Life lessons. Elisabeth Kubler-Ross and David Kessler.

2   The serenity prayer is of uncertain origin, and has been attributed to various persons including Francis of Assisi, Friedrich Oetinger (an eighteenth century theologian) and Reinhold Niebuhr (a twentieth century theologian).

3   p3. Loving what is. Byron Katie.

4   p25. Becoming human. Jean Vanier.

5   p25-6. Ibid.

6   Oxford encyclopaedic dictionary.

7   Collins junior illustrated dictionary.

8   p119. Mastering life's energies. Maria Nemeth.

9   p327. How people grow. Cloud and Townsend.

CHAPTER 5

1   p95-6. Mastering life's energies. Maria Nemeth.

2   p96. Ibid.

3   p143. Growing leaders. James Lawrence.

4   p9. The artist's way. Julia Cameron.

CHAPTER 6

1   p59. Becoming human. Vanier.

2   p118. Finding sanctuary. Abbot Christopher Jamison.

3   p58-9. Vanier.

4   p10ff. The divine matrix. Greg Braden.

5   p41. Vanier.

6   p130. Ibid.

7   p58. Finding happiness. Abbot Christopher Jamison.

8   p58. Ibid.

9   see 'Workshop' notes, 03.03.5, 1993-4.

NOTES

10   Quoted p108. Mastering life's energies. Maria Nemeth.
11   According to the Online etymology dictionary, the word
     'relationship' first appeared in 1744 but was not used to
     denote a specifically romantic tie until 1944.
12   Online etymology dictionary.
13   p9. Finding sanctuary. Abbot Christopher Jamison.
14   p19-20. The way of the heart. Henri Nouwen.
15   p 40. Vanier.
16   p116. Finding sanctuary. Abbot Christopher Jamison.

CHAPTER 7
1   Day 23 in 'The purpose driven life' by Rick Warren deals
     with this issue.
2   The divine matrix. Gregg Braden. A fascinating and
     accessible book looking at the scientific basis for the
     connectedness of all things in a way that bridges time and
     space.

CHAPTER 8
1   p40. Mastering life's energies. Maria Nemeth.
2   p2. The intention experiment. Lynne McTaggart.
3   Over the last thirty years or so a vast number of experiments
     have been conducted around the world to look at the subject
     of intention. In these experiments, intention is defined as 'a
     purposeful plan to perform an action, which will lead to a
     desired outcome.' These experiments have conclusively
     demonstrated that 'thinking certain thoughts can affect one's
     own body, inanimate objects and virtually all manner of
     living things, from single celled organisms to human beings'
     (p12-13ff. The intention experiment. Lynne Mc Taggart).
4   p40. Nemeth.

CHAPTER 9
1   p93. The divine matrix. Greg Braden.

2   Quoted p27. A season for the Spirit. Martin L Smith.

3   p27. Ibid.

4   p20-21. Ibid.

5   p222. How people grow. Cloud and Townsend.

6   p3. Loving what is. Byron Katie.

7   p305. How people grow. Cloud and Townsend.

8   p222. Ibid.

9   p20. Healing for damaged emotions. David Seamands.

10   p40. Mastering life's energies. Maria Nemeth.

CHAPTER 10

1   Pilgrim's progress. John Bunyan.

2   p49-50. Jonathan Edwards, America's genius. Christian Timothy George.

3   p85. Finding sanctuary. Abbot Christopher Jamison.

4   p89. Ibid.

5   Thomas Merton, quoted p84 ibid.

6   Westminster larger catechism, question 1.

CHAPTER 11

1   p126. Mentoring for spiritual growth. Tony Horsfall.

2   p55. The way of the heart. Henri Nouwen.

3   p67. Awareness. Anthony De Mello.

4   John Calvin's argument, quoted p35-36. Sacred companions. David Benner.

5   p106. Horsfall.

6   p56-7. Ibid.

7   p39. Ibid.

FURTHER READING

CHAPTER 1
Transitions: making sense of life's changes. William Bridges.
Finding yourself in transition. Robert Brumet.

CHAPTER 2
Choosing to grow through life. Mike Breen.
How people grow. Henry Cloud and John Townsend.

CHAPTER 3
Managing your emotions. Erwin Lutzer.
Healing for damaged emotions. David Seamands.

CHAPTER 4
Deeper. Debbie Alsdorf.
Loving what is. Byron Katie.

CHAPTER 5
Change your questions, change your life. Marilee Adams.
Mastering life's energies. Maria Nemeth.

CHAPTER 6
Finding happiness. Abbot Christopher Jamison.
Becoming human. Jean Vanier.

CHAPTER 7
Choosing to grow through life. Mike Breen.
The purpose driven life. Rick Warren.

CHAPTER 8
Life lessons. Elisabeth Kubler-Ross and David Kessler.
Mastering life's energies. Maria Nemeth.

CHAPTER 9
Loving what is. Byron Katie.
How people grow. Dr Henry Cloud and Dr John Townsend.

CHAPTER 10
Finding sanctuary: monastic steps for everyday life. Abbott Christopher Jamison.
Pilgrim's progress. John Bunyan.

CHAPTER 11
Awareness. Anthony De Mello.
Sacred companions. David Benner.

BIBLIOGRAPHY

Adams, Marilee. Change your questions, change your life.

Alsdorf, Debbie. Deeper.

Benner, David. Sacred companions.

Braden, Greg. The divine matrix.

Breen, Mike. Choosing to grow through life.

Bridges, William. Managing transitions.

Bridges, William. Transitions: making sense of life's changes.

Brumet, Robert. Finding yourself in transition.

Bunyan, John. Pilgrim's progress.

Cameron, Julia. The artist's way.

Chester, Tim. The ordinary hero.

Cloud, Henry and Townsend, John. How people grow.

de Mello, Anthony. Awareness.

George, Christian Timothy. Jonathan Edwards, America's genius.

Horsfall, Tony. Mentoring for spiritual growth.

Jamison, Abbot Christopher. Finding happiness.

Jamison, Abbot Christopher. Finding sanctuary: monastic steps
    for everyday life.

Katie, Byron. Loving what is.

Kubler-Ross, Elisabeth and Kessler, David. Life lessons.

Lawrence, James. Growing leaders.

Lucado, Max. The song of the king.

Lutzer, Erwin. Managing your emotions.

McTaggart, Lynne. The intention experiment.

Nemeth, Maria. Mastering life's energies.

Nouwen, Henri. The way of the heart.

Pert, Candace. Molecules of emotion.

Seamands, David. Healing for damaged emotions.

Smith, Martin. A season for the spirit.

St John, Patricia. Treasures of the snow.

Vanier, Jean. Becoming human.

Warren, Rick. The purpose driven life.

Circle Books

Circle is a symbol of infinity and unity. It's part of a growing list of imprints, including o-books.net and zero-books.net.

Circle Books aims to publish books in Christian spirituality that are fresh, accessible, and stimulating.

Our books are available in all good English language bookstores worldwide. If you can't find the book on the shelves, then ask your bookstore to order it for you, quoting the ISBN and title. Or, you can order online—all major online retail sites carry our titles.

To see our list of titles, please view www.Circle-Books.com, growing by 80 titles per year.

Authors can learn more about our proposal process by going to our website and clicking on Your Company > Submissions.

We define Christian spirituality as the relationship between the self and its sense of the transcendent or sacred, which issues in literary and artistic expression, community, social activism, and practices. A wide range of disciplines within the field of religious studies can be called upon, including history, narrative studies, philosophy, theology, sociology, and psychology. Interfaith in approach, Circle Books fosters creative dialogue with non-Christian traditions.

And tune into MySpiritRadio.com for our book review radio show, hosted by June-Elleni Laine, where you can listen to authors discussing their books.

MySpiritRadio